# AMELIA

'A story that is memorable. Marvellous
description. It is a tremendous read
and I warmly recommend it.'

*Robert Dunbar,* 'The Gay Byrne Show'

**Special Merit Award to The O'Brien Press
from Reading Association of Ireland**
*'for exceptional care, skill and professionalism in
publishing, resulting in a consistently high standard in all
of the children's books published by The O'Brien Press'*

SIOBHÁN PARKINSON is one of the most highly acclaimed children's writers in Ireland. She has won numerous awards and her books have been translated into several languages, including French, German, Italian, Portuguese, Spanish and Danish. Siobhán lives in Dublin with her husband Roger, a woodturner, and their son Matthew, Siobhán's personal literary critic.

**OTHER BOOKS BY SIOBHÁN PARKINSON**

For younger readers

*Cows are Vegetarians*

*Animals Don't Have Ghosts*

*The Leprechaun Who Wished He Wasn't*

For older readers

*No Peace for Amelia*

*Sisters ... no way!*

*Four Kids, Three Cats, Two Cows, One Witch (maybe)*

*The Moon King*

*Call of the Whales*

*The Love Bean*

*Breaking the Wishbone*

# AMELIA

*Siobhán Parkinson*

THE O'BRIEN PRESS
DUBLIN

First published 1993 by The O'Brien Press Ltd,
20 Victoria Road, Rathgar, Dublin 6, Ireland.
Tel: +353 1 4923333; Fax: +353 1 4922777
E-mail: books@obrien.ie
Website: www.obrien.ie
Reprinted 1994, 1995, 1999, 2000, 2002.

ISBN 0-86278-352-6

British Library Cataloguing-in-Publication Data
A catalogue reference for this title is available
from the British Library.

6  7  8  9  10
02  03  04  05  06

The O'Brien Press receives
assistance from

Typesetting, layout, editing, design: The O'Brien Press Ltd
Illustration on page 3: Katharine White
Printing: Cox & Wyman Ltd

*To my mother*

**Acknowledgement**

Thanks to the Pearson family, especially
Siobhán Pearson, for help with historical detail.

*Author's note*

This story is set in Dublin in 1914, before the outbreak of the First World War. Many of the characters are Quakers, and for the sake of authenticity I have given them genuine Irish Quaker surnames. However, no reference is intended to any actual Dublin families, and any resemblance, apart from surname, between these characters and real people, living or dead, is entirely coincidental.

# CONTENTS

## BOOK I

## BOOK II

# BOOK I

# Teatime in Kenilworth Square

The raindrops made little silvery pings as they hit the bottom of the metal buckets that Amelia had set to catch them, so that she wouldn't have to sit and watch the floor all muddying and puddling. She'd found a dry spot to sit in, in a lumpy old armchair her mother had banished from the drawing room, and she'd kicked off her boots and drawn her stockinged feet up under her pinafore.

Sometimes, when she had to sit very still and quiet – at Meeting on Sundays, for instance, when you had to think godly thoughts and attend upon the Spirit, as Grandmama solemnly put it – Amelia would long to jump up and run around and make a rumpus. She had to concentrate very hard on just not fidgeting.

But when she had a plan she wanted to think about, Amelia found sitting still no problem at all. She could sit for ages and just think and imagine and work things out in her head. This is what she was doing now.

As she sat, she looked up at the streaming roof. It was a funny sensation to look up into the rain and not get wet. You could see the rain slithering quickly along the roof, and gathering at a corner to gush down in a splashy waterfall onto the garden path.

This was the room Amelia liked best in the house. In a

way, though, the orangery wasn't a room at all. It was a glass structure that you entered through elegant french doors from the dining room, at the back of the house. It had a black and white diamond-patterned tiled floor. It was more like part of the garden, really, than part of the house, because everywhere you looked, all you could see was sky and garden – apple trees and damson trees, sad and dripping today, and a long stretch of lawn leading to a garden bench, which stood, wet and lonely, against a red-brick wall. Even if you looked back into the house, you couldn't really see in. You could only see the garden reflected back at you in the glass panels of the french doors.

When Amelia's grandpapa had built the orangery at the end of the nineteenth century, some years before Amelia herself was born, it had been very fashionable. People really did grow oranges in orangeries in those days. Ornamental ones, of course – you couldn't expect to grow edible oranges in the Irish climate, even if you had the most beautiful orangery in Rathgar.

Amelia often imagined what the orangery would have looked like then. In fact, she thought she could just remember it as it had been when she was much younger. There had been bamboo furniture and smart little orange trees in spick-and-span tubs, globes of shiny dark leaves clustered on top of slender trunks, with here and there a miniature fruit glowing among the foliage. The whole glass pavilion had been filled with light and scented with a sweet citrus tang.

But the orangery had fallen into disuse since Grandpapa's death. 'Vainglory,' Grandmama had pronounced one day, standing in the orangery and shaking her head sorrowfully. Amelia had been too small to know what that meant, but it sounded rather wonderful. And then somehow all the lovely slender bamboo furniture with its exotic leopard-like markings had disappeared, and goodness knows what had happened to the orange trees.

After that, the orangery was simply left to moulder. The glass was grimy now, and Mick Moriarty, the outdoor man who looked after the garden and cleaned the gutters and mended the roof, kept his tools in it, and odd pieces of furniture that people wanted to get rid of from other rooms in the house found their way there. And of course Amelia used it as her special place when she wanted to get away for a quiet think and to look at the sky. Not that you could hide very well in it, because it was all open and bright, but for some reason people didn't seem to think of looking for her there, and Amelia often managed a whole hour or more on her own in her special inside-outside place.

Mama would peer into the orangery from time to time from the dining room and make vague promises out loud to herself about clearing it out, but then she would close the lace curtains that hung before the french doors, and forget all about it again. Mama was like that. She thought that if she spoke grimly enough to herself about the necessity of attending to little household tasks, they were as good as done, and then she was free to get on with her real life, as she called it.

Amelia had mixed feelings about her mother's mutterings. Of course she would have liked to see the orangery restored to its former splendour, with the orange trees reinstated in their vainglorious tubs, the leaky roof mended and the floor polished and gleaming again. But at the same time, she didn't like the idea of a spring-cleaning. That would make people remember the orangery, and they might start to regard it as a place where any of the family might sit on spring afternoons, doing their beastly darning or reading their rotten old books and magazines or even scratching away with their fountain pens writing their unspeakable letters and making dull grown-uppish conversation about nothing at all, and it wouldn't be Amelia's special place any more.

But for now, it was still the last place anyone thought of looking, and that afternoon Amelia sat so long and so still in the sagging old chair, listening to the rainy music, that when she finally stood up because it must surely be teatime, she had pins and needles in her foot and she had to put it down on the floor very gently and hold her breath until the delicious but almost unbearable tingling stopped and she could put her weight on it and prise it into her boot.

Then she did up her laces quickly, slipped through the french doors back into the house and arrived in the drawing room just as Mary Ann brought in the tea-tray.

A huge fire was blazing in the drawing-room grate, and an occasional raindrop found its way down the chimney and spat and fizzled as it hit the flames and died. Grandmama sat in her usual straight-backed chair beside the fire, doing her cross-stitch. 'Love thy neighbour,' was the motto on her sampler, and some modest little wildflowers wound through the lettering.

Amelia's younger brother Edmund lay on his tummy on the hearthrug, waving his feet in the air. He must have been playing trains because he was making tiresome chugging and puffing noises. Amelia never took much notice of Edmund, but you couldn't ignore him entirely, because he made a great deal of noise for such a small boy.

'Oh, do be quiet, Edmund,' said Amelia automatically, for this was what she always said as soon as she caught sight of him anywhere about the house.

'Shan't!' said Edmund, just as automatically, and without looking up from his game.

'Children! Children!' said Grandmama, also automatically, and Amelia went over to her corner to give the old lady a kiss. 'Sorry, Grandmama,' she murmured into the old lady's ear. Her face smelt of tea and rosewater, as it always did, and her old cheek was dry and soft.

Amelia's grandmama wore an old-fashioned plain dress that buttoned up the front like a shirt. This wasn't just because she was an old lady, and old ladies can't be expected to keep up with the fashions, but because she had always dressed that way, as all Quaker ladies had done in her youth. Nowadays, even the most pious Quaker ladies wore whatever they chose, but some of the very oldest ones still clung to the old way of dress.

Grandmama poured the tea into large white teacups for herself and Amelia. Cook had sent up a glass of Jersey milk for Edmund, who was too young for tea. And there was brown bread and butter, white bread and butter and a plate of warm scones and a glass dish of strawberry jam. Grandmama put the plate of scones by the fire, to keep warm until all the bread and butter was eaten, for you weren't allowed to have any scones until then.

Edmund sat up and drank his milk carefully. He had only just been promoted from nursery tea in the schoolroom to family tea in the drawing room, and he didn't want to be sent back, so for once he kept quiet and sat still, all except for his feet, which he couldn't resist swinging softly under his chair.

The children had almost worked their way through the bread and butter and were about to ask Grandmama if they might have a scone, when Mama breezed in, bringing a swirl of cold air and a small shower of raindrops with her.

'Oh, I'm just in time!' she laughed, stuffing her single glove into her coat pocket and shaking more raindrops out of her coat as she swung out of it and sat down. (Mama generally left the house with two gloves, but she rarely returned with two.) As she took off her dripping hat, a large lock of dark hair came loose and hung down the side of her face. Mama swept it aside impatiently, not bothering to pin it back up again, as anyone else's mama would have done. She tossed her hat onto the ottoman in a way that Amelia would never have got away with, and alternately blew on her fingers and held them out to the fire, as if she didn't know perfectly well that that was a sure way to get chilblains.

'Well, not quite in time,' said Grandmama, who had a fine respect for the truth, 'but not quite late either.' Amelia and Edmund watched in consternation as Mama tucked into the scones and jam straight away without having to go through the bread-and-butter course.

Amelia's mama was a great disappointment to Amelia in many ways. Though she didn't dress as plainly as Grandmama, still she took no trouble at all, and went about the house in an old blue serge thing that Amelia couldn't abide. Sometimes Amelia had to remind her to change out of it if she was going out or expecting company, and then she would drag on her grey silk, which was dull but at least had the advantage of being nicely cut and of a good quality material.

Amelia was too young for real frocks. She wore drab dresses with buttoned cuffs and neat little collars under her everyday pinafores, and even for Sunday she only had a dull tartan with no sash. But that was all about to change. For soon Amelia would be not a little girl but a Young Lady, and that meant good frocks and fine stockings and putting her hair up. She would soon be thirteen, and that was almost fourteen, and at fifteen one could certainly put one's hair up. For the moment, it hung in yellow and brass streaks down her back and was pinned behind her ears so that you could see how they stuck out, to Amelia's great grief.

Mama didn't even notice Grandmama's little reproof. 'Tea's cold!' she spluttered on her first gulp.

'Shall I ring for a fresh pot, Mama?' asked Amelia primly,

practising for being a Young Lady.

'Well ...' Mama looked at Grandmama doubtfully, for it was a family rule not to make life difficult for the servants. 'Well, I'll tell you what, why don't you run down to the kitchen yourself, and save Mary Ann a trip, darling?'

'Yes, Mama,' said Amelia.

She closed the door behind her carefully, because she would have slammed it if she hadn't tried very hard not to. Amelia was cross with Mama. Here she was as usual, whirling in late to meals, looking like something the cat brought in – and with only one glove again – and then expecting Amelia to be her serving girl and run errands for her. Well, all this would have to change when Amelia became a Young Lady.

But in the meantime, little girls had to be seen and not heard, and Amelia would simply have to put up with it.

Although it was only just after five o'clock, it was quite dark at the back of the house, because of the grey weather outside. Amelia had to peer to see the stone steps that led down to the kitchen.

The kitchen was warm but gloomy. The kitchen lamps were never lit until six, whatever the weather. But it smelt good there. Cook had started on the dinner already, although the grown-ups didn't dine until eight. Steak and kidney pudding, it must be, because Amelia could smell the kidneys frying and Cook was rolling out pastry. The children had their dinner at one o'clock. They had a cup of cocoa going to bed, but tea was their last meal of the day, and Amelia often felt envious of the grown-ups when she smelt the good warm cooking smells in the evening.

There was no sign of Mary Ann. She must be in the scullery, peeling potatoes or scrubbing saucepans.

'Could we have a hot drop, please, Cook?' asked Amelia politely, putting the teapot on the kitchen table. 'You see, Mama was late and the tea was cold.'

'Certainly, my dear,' said Cook. 'But will you ask Mary Ann to get it? My hands are all flour. She's out in the scullery.'

The scullery was cold after the warmth of the kitchen with its big hot range, and was even darker than the kitchen.

'Mary Ann?' said Amelia into the chilly gloom. She could hear the rain whooshing down the drainpipe outside the back door. She felt a bit shy addressing Mary Ann, who was new. She and Amelia had never had a conversation before.

'Oh lawny!' yelped Mary Ann, dropping a saucepan onto the black flagged floor with a terrible clatter. She had been humming to herself as she worked, and what with the noise of the rain and the roar of the fire in the kitchen chimney, she mustn't have heard Amelia's approach.

'I'm sorry I made you jump,' said Amelia stiffly, to Mary Ann's stooped back. 'I'm Amelia Pim.' And she held out her hand in the semi-darkness.

Mary Ann straightened up with the retrieved saucepan in her hand and peered at Amelia. Amelia stared back. She had never seen such a very angular girl before. Mary Ann looked younger than Amelia, and was much thinner. She seemed to be all elbows and legs, and she held her arms out at an angle from her skinny body as if she were about to lurch into awkward flight at any moment.

Mary Ann mustn't have seen Amelia's outstretched hand. At any rate, she didn't take any notice of it. Instead, she burst into peals of laughter. 'Are you indeed?' she asked heartily, but Amelia understood from her tone that it wasn't a real question. 'And I'm the Queen of Sheba!' she added with another laugh.

'Oh!' said Amelia, not quite sure how to respond to this piece of information.

'Only I'm in disguise, see? I'm running away from my father, the evil Tsar, who wants to lock me up in a nunnery for the rest of my days, and I'm in hiding here in Dublin. My name in exile is Mary Ann Maloney. Pleased to make your acquaintance.'

'I thought the Tsar was in Russia,' Amelia managed at last. 'Not Sheba.'

'Oh, you don't want to believe everything you hear,' said Mary Ann darkly. 'And what can I do for your ladyship?'

'Oh, I'm not a ladyship.'

'Well, I know that,' retorted Mary Ann. 'It's just a manner of speaking, so it is. A turn of phrase, don't you know.'

'Oh,' said Amelia, for the third time. What a strange girl this was! Amelia wondered if she mightn't be a bit, you know, funny in the head or something. She didn't know much about servants, although they'd been around her all her life. She had been brought up always to be polite and kind to them, but it never occurred to her that she might have a normal conversation with one, apart from asking for something or thanking them for something. Not that this was a very normal conversation. On the whole, Amelia preferred her conversations to be normal.

'Could I have a pot of tea, please?' she asked.

'Indeed and you could, Miss Amelia,' said Mary Ann, in a much more normal, servantish sort of voice.

'Oh, just Amelia, please. Not Miss. It's a sort of principle with us, you see.'

'What is?' asked Mary Ann, moving into the kitchen and setting about making the tea. Cook was nowhere to be seen, but Amelia could hear her rattling about in the pantry.

'Not to use titles like Miss or Mister,' explained Amelia. 'Because we're Friends, you see.'

'Oh, I'm sure we are, Miss Amelia, the best of friends, but all the same, if you don't mind, I know my place and I like to keep in it. Just because I make a little joke every now and again, it doesn't mean I don't know how to behave to my betters, thank you very much.'

'Oh, not that sort of friends, I didn't mean that. I meant it's against our religion.'

Now it was Mary Ann's turn to wonder if Amelia wasn't a bit soft in the head. Blathering on about Russia, saying they were friends and in the next breath seeming to change her mind about it, and now it seemed that something was against this girl's religion. Mary Ann was blowed if she knew what exactly it was that was supposed to be against her religion, but she thought it best just to go along with her. Other people's religion could be a touchy subject.

'Whatever you say, Miss.' Mary Ann adjusted the cosy around the teapot again and handed it back to Amelia. 'Mind your step now, Miss. It's getting dusk. Three steps up, remember. And don't bother with the door. I'll close it after you.'

And Mary Ann shook her head at Amelia's retreating back. She was beginning to wonder if this service lark was such a good idea. She had very nearly landed a nice little job in Mr Murphy's grocer's shop not half-a-mile from her own front door, and she might have been there now at this very minute among the jars and the tins and the sacks of meal and flour, weighing out sugar into nice neat bags and learning to twist a brown-paper poke for a ha'porth of boiled sweets and living at home with her Ma and her Da and the little ones and not having to sleep in an iron bed all by herself and talk to rich folks and polish their silver and scrub their saucepans.

But then Mr Murphy had got a boy who wanted to be apprenticed to the trade, and who could blame the elderly grocer for preferring a strong lad willing to serve his time to a slip of a girl who didn't know a pennyweight from a bushel of oats and might be off getting married and having babies before she could write a receipt?

In bed that night Amelia once more took her plan out of the drawer she had put it in at the back of her mind at teatime and shook it out to think about it some more. She liked to do that, unfolding it carefully and turning it this way and that and admiring it as various thoughts and ideas fell on it and lit it from this angle or that. But she couldn't settle to thinking about her plan properly. Every time she tried to picture the dress, for example – cherry red silk, with a big sash and a flounce at the hem – other things kept floating into her head and pushing it aside. It had been rather an eventful afternoon after all.

Papa had come home to tea, which was unusual for him, bursting in out of the rain just as Amelia was coming back from the kitchen with the teapot and wondering if maybe Mary Ann was suffering from delusions – there *was* such a thing, you know.

Unlike Mama, Papa shook his umbrella out in the porch and then stood it in the drip tray in the umbrella stand and took off his greatcoat in the hall and hung it up carefully on its peg on the hallstand. The Pims didn't have a manservant to open the door and look after the coats. They considered this 'excessive'. The grown-ups in Amelia's family considered a lot of things excessive, to Amelia's mortification.

'My princess!' cried Papa, and Amelia knew that if she hadn't been carrying a nuisance of a hot teapot he would have swung her off her feet in a big bear-hug. Instead, he took the teapot from her, kissed her on the forehead and swung open the door to the drawing room. Both of Amelia's parents made a great deal of coming into a room. You certainly knew when they were around.

Amelia adored her papa. He was tall, and fair-haired like her, only that, unlike hers, his hair curled magnificently, and his face was big and brown and his eyes sharp and blue and his voice deep and cheerful, and he told jokes. He dressed elegantly and carefully, and he never lost his gloves. And he had a big fair moustache that he fingered when he was thinking.

Amelia's papa was an importer and merchant. He dealt mostly in fine wines and tea, and he did some business also in spices and foreign produce. He had a depot at the docks where the goods he had bought from Ceylon and Brazil and Madagascar and France and Siam were stashed in tea-chests and wooden trunks and metal boxes. The depot smelt warm and fruity and spicy – it smelt of Christmas even in June. And he had warehouses and stores and cellars in several places in town where the tea was blended and the wines were stacked and aged. He had an office in town too, where he did long complicated sums in enormous ledgers and he thought out plans and strategies and hired workers and commissioned ships and barges and made telephone calls to distant places and where, no doubt, he kept large piles of money – maybe even gold – in strongboxes and safes.

Amelia was proud of her papa. He made lots of money, she knew, for there was always enough and nobody ever worried about it. He was a bit like Grandpapa, she thought, who had built the orangery, and whom Amelia could remember only dimly. He didn't read as many books as Mama, and he only went to Meeting occasionally, to Grandmama's chagrin, but he was a fine papa and he always said Amelia was his favourite daughter. He had only one daughter, of course, but he didn't ever say Edmund was his favourite son, so Amelia knew he really meant that she was his favourite child, although he couldn't say so outright for fear of offending Edmund.

'Mama!' cried Papa as he strode into the drawing room with the teapot, as if he were terribly surprised to see her. He meant Grandmama, of course, who was his mama. And he put the teapot down and bent to kiss the old lady. She said nothing, but went on stitching her sampler. 'Roberta,' he said to Mama in a soft voice, as she handed him a cup of tea.

'Do have a scone, Papa,' insisted Amelia. 'They're deliciously fresh, and they won't be half so good tomorrow and the jam's strawberry, your favourite kind.'

'What brings you home so early, Charles?' asked Mama.

'Petrol power!' answered Papa with a beam.

'Charles! You haven't! We agreed we wouldn't! Oh, is it very beautiful? Oh Charles, you shouldn't. It's excessive. We don't need it. There's the tram, and we have the landau. Oh, Charles!' Mama was standing up and sitting down again and smiling and looking cross at the same time.

'What are you talking about?' asked Amelia. 'What's excessive?'

'It's not excessive at all,' said Papa. 'It's perfectly sensible. Lots of people have motor-cars now. It's much quicker. It's the modern way to travel, Roberta. And we haven't really got the landau. One or other of those horses is always lame. They're old – beyond it. It was either this or buy a pair of horses. This was much the cheaper option, when you consider the price of feeding a pair of horses.'

Clip and Clop, the aged horses, would probably be sold now. But no-one stopped to think of such unpleasantness, not this afternoon amid such excitement.

'Oh, Papa, Papa!' the children cried together. 'A motor-car! Where is it? Can we see? Can we have a ride?'

'It's out on the road, of course. You didn't expect me to drive it up the garden path and into the house, did you?'

So they all scrambled into their outdoor things, tea and scones and strawberry jam completely forgotten, and put up their umbrellas and tumbled down the front steps and through the garden into the road to look at the new car.

It was magnificent! It gleamed and shone, even in the rain,

and its lights were like two great eyes out in front. The hood was up because of the rain, but you could see the leather upholstery inside and the bodywork was a shining dark green. Papa wouldn't agree to take anyone for a spin this afternoon, because, he said, the filthy weather made it difficult to drive, but he promised them all a go as soon as the rain cleared up.

Only Grandmama didn't beg to go for a drive. She stood at the hall-door and shook her head. Amelia could just hear what she said: 'Vainglory!'

And that was the reason that Amelia couldn't concentrate properly on her own thoughts that night. Her head was full of Papa and the magnificent new motor-car. At last she had something to boast of to her friends. They all had more finery and more extensive wardrobes, more servants and bigger houses, more outings and more holidays than Amelia's family, and their mamas had people to tea and gave garden parties in the summer and weren't eternally rushing around forming leagues for this and committees against that. Most of them had finer carriages than the Pims, and some already had motor-cars, but none, Amelia was convinced, had a car as handsome and as sleek and as dashing as her papa's.

Before she knew it, Amelia was drifting into a dream where Grandpapa, in his old-fashioned high collar and dark suit was driving the motor-car through the orangery, with Mama waving a single sodden glove at him and Mary Ann shouting over the din, 'Make way for the Queen of Sheba!'

# Women and Ladies

Amelia often helped her mother with her circulars, especially if there was nothing better to do. Edmund wanted to help too. 'What are circulars, Mama?' he asked.

'Oh, you know, just papers, darling. I don't think you'd be a bit interested.'

'Oh, Mama, Mama, I would, I would! Please, Mama!' Edmund had a very whiney voice that irritated Amelia. Mama said his voice was thin and piping because he was still very small, and that Amelia shouldn't let it irritate her, but Amelia knew that he put on that special whine expressly to annoy her.

Amelia had visions of Edmund getting sticky finger marks all over the papers and gumming the envelopes together and making a complete mess of everything, but she knew she mustn't point this out to Mama, as that would only make Mama take Edmund's side, as if she didn't always anyway.

But when Edmund saw just how dull doing the circulars was, he soon trotted off, trailing his wooden train engine, clickety-clack, clickety-clack, across the morning-room floor, bump, over the door saddle and into the hall, which was the best place for playing Edmund's sort of games, because it was long and free of furniture. 'I thought you meant circles,' he complained, turning back to look at them from the doorway. 'Making paper moons, I thought.'

'Oh, the sweetie,' whispered Mama with a foolish smile on her face as the door closed behind the little boy. 'Did you hear, Amelia? He thought we were cutting paper shapes. Oh, remind me to tell Papa. The little darling.'

Amelia didn't answer. She went on doggedly folding the circulars and piling them up for Mama to stuff into the envelopes. 'Votes for Women!' it said in big black letters on the circulars. When they were all folded and in their envelopes, Mama would address them in her small, neat handwriting. Amelia never could understand why Mama's handwriting was so neat, when everything else about her was so sloppy and disorganised. Then Amelia would stamp them all, lining up the king's head with the corner of each envelope. She liked that bit. The king looked grave and handsome on the stamps.

They did ever so many circulars, and Amelia got very tired and bored. 'Why do you want votes for women, Mama?' she asked, not because she really wanted to know, but just for something to say.

'Why, Amelia, what a question!' said Mama, pausing for a moment to look at her daughter, as if she was wondering where on earth she had got her from.

'Well, why?' asked Amelia again, this time more defiantly. She didn't like it when Mama looked at her in that way, as if she didn't know her.

'Well, because it's not fair that only men should be allowed to vote, Amelia. Surely you can see that? It's against natural justice.'

'Yes,' said Amelia doubtfully. 'Yes, I see that it's fairer if everyone can vote. But why do you actually *want* to vote? And why should you want to be the one to change things? What's it got to do with us, Mama?'

'What's it got to do with us? But we're women, Amelia.'

What a peculiar thing to say! Nobody had ever called Amelia a woman before. She looked up at Mama. 'Oh,' she said. 'Aren't we ladies, Mama?'

'Well, yes, we are, I suppose.' Mama didn't sound too happy to called a lady. 'Yes, we are ladies by rank and social position, Amelia.'

'And by behaviour, Mama,' added Amelia virtuously.

'Yes, I hope so, that too. But first and foremost we are women. That comes first.'

'Is it better to be a woman or a lady, Mama?'

'It isn't a question of better. It is a very fine thing to be a woman, Amelia. It just happens that the way things are, some women are lucky enough to be ladies too.'

'So we are lucky women, Mama.'

'Yes, dear, very lucky.'

'So why do we need the vote then?'

'Amelia! I've just explained that it's not fair. It's a question of justice.'

'But it's not fair either that we're ladies and some women aren't, is it?'

Just at that moment, Mary Ann arrived to clear out the grate. She was carrying a metal bucket and a shovel for the ashes. 'Sorry, Ma'am,' she said. 'I thought the room was free.' And she was just about to poke herself back out the door as quickly as she had bobbed in.

'Oh no, Mary Ann,' said Mama. 'Don't mind us. Come on in and get on with your work. We may be ages yet.'

'Would you like to be a lady, Mary Ann?' asked Amelia.

'Amelia!' hissed Mama.

'It's all right, Ma'am,' said Mary Ann, cheerfully shovelling the ashes and cinders into the bucket. 'She hasn't a titter of wit, Miss Amelia hasn't. But I don't mind a bit. Can't afford to, can I?'

'Well said, Mary Ann,' said Mama admiringly. 'Spoken

like a true-hearted woman.'

But Amelia thought Mary Ann was cruel to say such things. She didn't know her place, that girl. And now she was trying to turn Amelia's mother against her. Amelia felt tears aching in her throat, but she swallowed and said gaily, 'Would you like to have the vote, then, Mary Ann?'

'The vote!' Mary Ann laughed. 'What good would the vote be to the likes of me? Living in a country that's ruled by a foreign king *nobody* voted for, who's going to land us all in a war if we don't look out, and me with a family of little brothers and sisters to worry about, with me da out of work and me ma in bad health and me only older brother in prison.'

'Prison, Mary Ann!' Mama was all concern.

'Oh lawny, Ma'am!' wailed Mary Ann. 'I didn't mean to let that out. Ma'am, don't let on to the Master, will you, please, Ma'am? We're not a bad family, we're not. Honest, we're not. He's a political prisoner, Ma'am, I swear to God. He didn't do anything wicked. He's a good lad.'

Amelia looked at Mama. Mary Ann had sworn! That was not allowed in a Quaker household, under any circumstances, even as a turn of phrase. But Mama didn't reprimand Mary Ann at all.

'Don't worry about it, Mary Ann,' she said. 'I promise you it won't make any difference at all to your employment here. We will be concerned about it certainly, but only because we don't like to think of someone unjustly imprisoned. We don't think any the less of you for it. Please believe that.'

Well! Whatever Mama thought, Amelia wasn't too impressed to hear that they had the sister of a prisoner under their roof. She wondered what Papa would think.

But Amelia didn't get a chance to break the news about Mary Ann's brother to Papa, because Mama told him herself that evening when he came home from the office. Amelia had been saving it up to tell him, and looking forward to seeing his face when she announced it. Would he be surprised? Surely. Would he be angry? Perhaps. Would he denounce Mary Ann and throw her out of the house? That would be very thrilling, of course, but Amelia mustn't allow herself to think that. Even if Mary Ann's family was in disgrace, still, it wouldn't be gentlemanly of Papa to fling her down the porch steps and show her the garden gate. Perhaps he would just give her her notice quietly and pay her a week's wages and ask her to pack her things and leave by the back door. Yes, that's probably what he would do, Amelia thought. Then she allowed herself to think: Poor Mary Ann! She was a bit strange and she said ever such odd things, but even so, it wasn't nice to be dismissed from your situation.

As it happened, Amelia missed Papa's return. Edmund had a cold and had to go to bed early, which meant that Amelia had to go upstairs to read him his bedtime story before Papa got home. Mama had made him some chamomile tea, with lemon peel and honey. It smelt absolutely foul.

How would I feel if Edmund were in gaol? Amelia found herself thinking. Relieved was the first word that came into her head. But then she saw how very small and wretched he looked, sitting up in his nightshirt with an extra quilt around his shoulders, with his eyes streaming and streaming and his nose quite pink from blowing, sipping that awful yellow stuff Mama had made, and for just a fleeting moment Amelia felt like hugging him. But Mama had had a fire lit in his room, because of his cold, which was a lovely treat, so Amelia was determined not to be carried away by sympathy.

'You'll have to learn to read for yourself soon,' she warned him, as she did every night, though secretly she enjoyed the opportunity to re-read stories she remembered from when she was much younger.

'Yes, 'Melia,' snuffled Edmund meekly.

Edmund's room was at the back of the house, so Amelia didn't hear Papa's motor-car drawing up outside. By the time she came down to tell Mama that Edmund was ready to be tucked in, Papa was warming himself at the drawing-room fire.

'The poor lass,' Papa was saying.

For a moment, Amelia thought he meant her, having to read endless stories to an ungrateful little brother. But soon she realised he must mean Mary Ann, because Mama said, 'I can't get the full story out of her. I think he must be involved in the IRB, Charles. You know, we can't condone that sort of thing. Not if they are advocating armed rebellion.'

Good heavens! What was all this? Mama must have been talking to Mary Ann privately. And she hadn't mentioned it to Amelia!

'Of course not. But still, we must do everything we can for the family. It sounds as if the mother's in a bad way. Do you think it's ...'

Just then, the adults noticed that Amelia had joined them and was listening to every word they said, and in their tiresome way they immediately changed the subject. 'How's Edmund? Has he said his prayers?'

'He wants his goodnight kiss, Mama. And he's asking if Papa is home yet.'

Amelia sat on a tapestry footstool looking into the fire and puzzling over what she had overheard, while her parents went upstairs to tend to their shivering son. Papa hadn't seemed angry at all about Mary Ann. In fact, he had seemed concerned. Well, that was a good thing, wasn't it? Amelia supposed she should be glad that he hadn't been loud and angry. It would have been dreadful, really, if he had made a scene, and there would have been tension and unhappiness in the household.

Amelia shifted uneasily on the footstool. She had to admit, if she was honest, that a little part of herself would have enjoyed the drama if Papa had turned Mary Ann from the house. Amelia shuddered at herself. Was she a truly hateful person, to be thinking such thoughts? She couldn't bear to think so ill of herself. No, she decided. No, she wouldn't have wanted Papa to be nasty to Mary Ann. No, really, that would have been too awful.

But, still, a little demon inside Amelia went on thinking unworthy thoughts. Wouldn't it have been fun if Papa had wanted to turn Mary Ann out, and Mama and Amelia, with tears in their eyes, had had to plead with him not to? Yes, that would have been, well, not fun exactly, but enjoyable.

Amelia shook herself again, horrified at her own nastiness. She resolved there and then that she would try to be a better person. Yes, she would make it up to Mary Ann. She would do her some little kindness, to prove to her that she, Amelia Pim, wasn't at all outraged by Mary Ann's unfortunate family circumstances. Unfortunate family circumstances. Yes, that sounded well. Mary Ann's family circumstances were unfortunate. That was the sort of thing Mama said. Perhaps Amelia should try to be a little more like Mama. In some ways at least.

# The Wisdom of Lucinda

Our maid's family circumstances are unfortunate,' Amelia whispered to her friend Lucinda Goodbody between Geography and Geometry next day at the Grosvenor Academy for Young Ladies.

'Oooh! Is she in trouble?' asked Lucinda. 'I mean, is she in the family way?'

Amelia wasn't sure what 'in the family way' meant, but it sounded appropriate. She nodded gravely. 'And Patrick's in prison,' she added.

'Oh dear,' said Lucinda, 'that means she can't get married so. Have you seen my set square?'

'Yes, you've used it as a bookmark, look. Can she not? Get married, I mean.'

'Well, not if he's in prison. They wouldn't allow it.'

Amelia was puzzled by this piece of information. Why should her brother's being in prison prevent Mary Ann from doing as she pleased? How very odd the world was, to be sure.

'No talking at the back, please,' said Miss Reddick, the mathematics teacher, pleasantly.

And the two girls said, 'Sorry, Miss Reddick.'

After Geometry was coffee break. Nobody ever had any coffee, of course, except the teachers. The children weren't allowed out to play, as it was only supposed to be a short break, just long enough to drink a cup of something. Some of the girls brought milk, in blue glass medicine bottles stopped with a cork. Mary Webb brought hers in a Baby Power bottle, which made them all laugh, because everyone knew that her father was a teetotaller. Mary protested that her mother bought a Baby Power every Christmas, but only for the plum pudding; still, the others teased her mercilessly all the same.

The girls who didn't bring milk queued up to get a drink from the drinking-water tap in the corridor.

'I don't think Mary Ann wants to get married anyway,' said Amelia, picking up her earlier conversation with Lucinda. 'She's very young.'

'Well, she should,' said Lucinda. 'They marry young anyway.'

'Who?'

'The lower orders.'

'What's that?'

'Servants,' said Lucinda. 'Poor people. They marry young and have too many babies. That's why they're poor.'

'Oh. Is it?'

'Of course, you ninny. Everyone knows that.'

'But you said just now that she should want to get married.'

'Yes, but that's because she's in the family way. That's different. You have to if you are.'

'Oh,' said Amelia again, feeling she was rather missing the point. This conversation was getting more and more confusing, so Amelia thought she would change the subject to one she had more control over.

'Can you keep a secret, Luce?'

Amelia didn't wait for her friend's answer. She had decided that the time had come to unveil her plan. 'I'm giving a party!' she said breathlessly.

'Oh goody!' Lucinda jumped up and down, waving the tin cup from the drinking fountain. But she found she couldn't wave it sufficiently dramatically, because it was chained to the wall, so she resorted to tapping on it with her slate-pencil. It made a pinging sound. 'Listen, everyone! Good news! Amelia Pim's giving a party! Better keep on her good side, everyone, or you won't get invited. Yippee!' And Lucinda lifted her pinafore above her knees and did a little jig on the spot.

All the girls laughed and clapped and crowded around. Somebody lilted a tune in time to Lucinda's steps. Lucinda was pretty and bubbly and had masses of wonderful auburn curls and was very popular. If she laughed about something, other people laughed too and said how funny it was, even if they hadn't found it funny before, and if she made a little scene like this, everyone flocked around and gave it their full attention. And so Amelia's plan, though it wasn't fully formed at all yet, was suddenly shot from obscurity into the full glare of the attention of half-a-dozen twelve- and thir-teen-year-old girls with nothing more interesting to look forward to than French verbs. And the funny thing was, Amelia didn't even mind, although she had asked Lucinda particularly to keep it a secret. It was lovely to be a source of excitement among the girls.

'Will there be young men, Amelia?' asked Dorothea Jacob slyly. Dorothea was terribly interested in the opposite sex and was for ever trying out new hairstyles, but she wasn't pretty like Lucinda, and people didn't like her much.

Amelia hadn't thought this far ahead at all. She stopped beaming, which she had been doing since she had, together with Lucinda, become the centre of attention, and she blushed. 'Eh, no,' she said nervously, for to tell the truth, she didn't know any.

'Ah!' sighed everyone.

'I mean, yes,' cried Amelia.

'Ah!' sighed everyone again, but this time in a completely different tone.

'And will we get a spin in your Papa's new motor?' asked Lucinda, her eyes shining. This was homage indeed, for Lucinda's father had been the first to acquire a motor-car, and for a long time Lucinda was held in extra special regard on this account.

'Of course!' cried Amelia. And a cheer went up, 'Hurrah!', which quite startled Mademoiselle Félicité who was scurrying from the staff sitting room, already several minutes late for class.

'Would you like to get married, Mary Ann?' Amelia asked the maid that afternoon, meeting her on the stairs.

'Married? I certainly would not like to get married!' said Mary Ann, dabbing a duster at the newel post as if she would like to knock it right off its pedestal. 'Haven't I enough family responsibilities? Anyway, why do you ask? Have you anyone in particular in mind?'

'Well, no,' Amelia admitted. 'I just thought maybe you were getting to an age when you might be thinking of it.'

'But I'm only fourteen!' exclaimed Mary Ann, taking another swipe at the newel post.

'Oh, well, then ...' said Amelia, who was startled to learn that Mary Ann was even that old. She wouldn't have put her above twelve. Really, though, she couldn't see what Lucinda had been thinking of, insisting that Mary Ann should be getting married.

'Maybe it's yourself that's starting to think about it,' suggested Mary Ann. 'Is that the way it is? Are you starting to get interested in the boys?'

'Boys!' Amelia practically spat the word out. As far as

Amelia was concerned, boys were nothing but trouble. They were loud and selfish and, in her experience, dirty. Small boys like Edmund were bad enough, with their silly noisy games and their endless whining and demands for stories and games of draughts, and as they got older they dabbled around with disgusting things like frogspawn and earwigs, and they seemed to keep useless quantities of string in their pockets and they blotted when they wrote and they put worms in the salad or spiders in the bath. Then when they were older still they wanted telescopes and footballs and airguns and the next thing you knew they were playing mucky games like polo and hockey, and they hadn't a clue about how to dress or make conversation. The only boys Amelia could abide were tame ones, who went to dancing classes, but these were hard to come by.

Mary Ann didn't press the point. The venom in Amelia's voice was enough to convince her that she was on the wrong track here. 'Keep your hair on!' she said. 'They are part of the human race, you know.'

'Huh!' said Amelia, as if she was not convinced on that last point. Then she remembered her resolution to be kind to Mary Ann. 'Oh, Mary Ann, let's go for a walk!'

'A walk, Miss!' Mary Ann sounded utterly astonished. 'But I can't go for a walk. I have work to do. It's after four already, and I'll have to get the tea soon, and then there's the dinner to help Cook with, and the fire in Master Edmund's bedroom to see to, and the drawing-room fire to check on, now I come to think of it, and ...'

'Goodness! Do you never get a rest, then?' asked Amelia.

'Yes, I do. After washing up after the dinner, me and Cook put our feet up and have a nice cup of cocoa, so we do, and a chat. It's my favourite part of the day. I really enjoy that cup of cocoa. Only sometimes, I do think of the little ones at home, who don't see cocoa from one end of the week to the other, and then sometimes I have to admit, Miss Amelia, I don't feel like finishing it, only I do, because I hate waste, and my ma hates waste and she brought me up like that. So for her sake, I drink it all up, even if it kills me.'

'Why don't they see cocoa, Mary Ann?'

'Because there isn't any. There isn't money for luxuries like cocoa. There's barely enough to pay the rent and pay for coal and food. Some weeks they do with less food because they've had to pay for fuel, and some days they don't light the fire at all, because there's no money left for fuel after buying in the food. And other times they try to dodge the landlord's agent who comes for the rent, in the hope that they could have both fuel and food for once. When I got this situation, Miss, it was the first time they were able to pay the rent, arrears and all, and still have enough for both fuel and food. But now the money I send home every week has to go for medicines, because my mother ...'

At this point, Mary Ann stopped for a moment, and there was a funny croaking sound in her throat. 'Because my mother ...' she tried again. Then she sat down on the stairs and put her head on her knees and a little high-pitched keening sound came from her, the like of which Amelia had never heard before. She couldn't be sure that Mary Ann was actually crying, because she couldn't hear sobs or snuffles, and her shoulders didn't heave at all.

Amelia stood for a moment looking at Mary Ann's spiky shoulder blades, which were hardly moving, and then she sank down on the stair beside her and put a tentative arm over those bony shoulders. 'What's wrong with your mother, Mary Ann?' she whispered. 'Is she ill?'

'Yes,' came the hoarse reply. Amelia could hardly hear Mary Ann, so she leant closer to the maid, until the fair head was touching the brown, and she patted Mary Ann as she had seen Mama pat Edmund when he hurt himself. 'It's consumption, Miss,' said Mary Ann in a very low voice.

'Is consumption very bad, Mary Ann?' asked Amelia.

'Yes, Miss. You die, Miss.'

'Oh, Mary Ann!' And Amelia felt a hot tear trickling down her own face.

She tried to imagine her own mama ill and dying, but though she could imagine Papa distraught with grief, and Grandmama silent in prayer, and Edmund whingeing and whining, and Dr Mitchell striding swiftly through the house with his black bag, she couldn't picture Mama at all. Her mother was fairly bouncing with health and energy. Amelia just couldn't imagine her weak and dependent, and she certainly couldn't imagine the house without her. Poor Mary Ann, Amelia thought.

And this time she meant it.

# Emerald Silk

Amelia and Mama were going to Clery's to buy material for the frock of Amelia's dreams. Amelia loved town, with all its hustle and bustle, and Clery's was her favourite place to go. The shop was very near the Pillar, where the trams started from. The trams all had little clanging bells, and they made clanking noises as they started off, and sometimes the conductors hung out at the back, shouting witticisms to their mates on other trams. Although Amelia admired her papa's car as a very handsome piece of machinery, and she was very proud to ride in it, really, if the truth were told, she preferred to travel by tram, where you could get a good look at your fellow-passengers and listen in to a few conversations. There were always women trying to juggle children and shopping, and old people tottering along the aisle and shaking their walking sticks at the conductor, and naughty little boys throwing lollipop sticks over the top rail, and families squabbling over who should sit on whose knee. Amelia always insisted on riding on the upper deck, if it wasn't raining. The trams were roofless, and it was a bit like riding on an open boat. She liked the view from up there, and sometimes the cherry trees in people's gardens snowed pink blossom on her hat and shoulders as she sailed by.

Mama and Papa had been mildly surprised to hear that

Amelia was giving a party.

'Are you, dear?' Mama had said in her exasperatingly vague way. 'How nice.'

The least Amelia had expected was whole-hearted opposition to her carefully hatched plan. But she didn't even get much interest. 'For my birthday, Mama,' she said slowly and carefully as if speaking to a small child or a deaf person.

'Of course, darling,' said Mama, looking up for a moment from a letter she was reading.

'I'm going to be thirteen in a few weeks, Mama,' said Amelia.

'Yes, dearest, I know how old you are. I was there when you were born, remember.'

Amelia blushed. This was just the sort of indelicate remark you could expect from Mama.

'So that's the reason for the party, Mama,' she went on, feeling as if she were swimming with all her clothes on or trying to walk through treacle in her gumboots.

'Well, of course. Amelia, my darling, why are you making such an *announcement* of all this? We always have a little tea-party in the schoolroom when one of you children has a birthday. Cook bakes one of her special Victoria sponges and she spends ages decorating it with curlicues and whirligigs and what-have-you, and sometimes your cousins from Chapelizod come, and maybe one or two girls from school, and we all sing Happy Birthday, and Edmund usually eats too much and has an upset tummy in the night.'

'Oh, Mama!' exclaimed Amelia. 'That's not the sort of party I mean. Not a *tea*-party. Not in the *school*room.'

'No?' said Mama, taking off her reading glasses and putting them down beside her plate.

Amelia automatically picked up the spectacles and put them in the little case where they lived, because she knew they would come to grief if she didn't. Mama was always losing her spectacles or else leaving them where someone sat on them or trod on them. They weren't likely to get trodden on on the breakfast table, but they could get smeared with butter or marmalade, or they might even get cleared away with the breakfast things and get taken to the kitchen.

'No,' said Amelia shortly, pouting at her reflection in the teapot.

'Well, what sort of party did you have in mind, Amelia?' asked Mama. 'You're a bit young for a ball, don't you think? And it's too cold for a garden party.'

'Just a *party* party, Mama. With streamers and pretty napkins and nice things to eat off trays and everyone in their best clothes and music. I know I'm too young for a ball, but we could have a dance or two, couldn't we?'

'Dancing! Amelia, are you serious?'

'Yes, of course I'm serious. A little dancing doesn't do any harm. We have all those tedious dancing lessons at school, don't we? Well, what's the point if we don't dance occasionally? It's as bad as learning all those awful French verbs even though we're never likely to meet a single French person ever in our lives and if we did, what could we say to them? "*J'aime, tu aimes, il aime* ..." Any sane French person would run a mile. And there's all that absurd geometry too. Who cares about the square on the hypotenuse, Mama? What difference is it going to make whether I can *prove* that it's equal to the sum of the squares on the other two sides? Isn't it enough that I *know* it is? Is it even worth knowing?'

'But it isn't,' intervened Papa, looking up over the top of *The Irish Times*, 'not unless it's a right-angled triangle. And you do know a single French person, or certainly I am led to believe that the instruction in French for which I pay not inconsiderable fees is administered by a lady of the French persuasion, and if I am mistaken in this, I shall be very annoyed with your headmistress.'

'Oh, Papa, you are so *hateful*!' said Amelia, and she burst into tears.

Even as she sniffed into her handkerchief, Amelia was rather shocked with herself for this outburst. She had never in her life called her papa hateful before. And he wasn't hateful at all; he was the kindest, handsomest, funniest papa in the world. At this thought Amelia wept even more fiercely into her hanky, and then she jumped up from her chair and ran to bury her face in Papa's waistcoat.

Papa put down his newspaper and laid his hand on her head. 'There, there, my princess, it's all right, it's all right.'

But this only made Amelia weep even more stormily. Why couldn't someone be mean and nasty to her, so that she could have a proper fight with them? What did they all mean by being so wretchedly *nice*?

'Poor 'Melia!' piped up Edmund in a wobbly voice. And then he burst into tears too, unnerved by the unaccustomed scene. So Mama had to take him on her knee and comfort him.

Papa gave Amelia his handkerchief, because hers was already sopping. It smelt of Sunlight soap and tobacco, which was Papa's own special smell.

Amelia knew she should apologise, but she didn't trust herself to say anything. If she opened her mouth, more wails might come out. So she said nothing, but did her best to mop up her face with Papa's hanky, and let a quiet little sob escape every now and then.

So Papa and Mama had agreed that if Amelia really wanted a party so badly, then she should have it. And if she wanted dancing, well then they would borrow a gramophone from somewhere and she could have music. 'Perhaps Grandmama might be persuaded to go to the country for a day or two,' said Papa, for everyone knew what Grandmama would think of something as frivolous as a party with dancing. Luckily, Grandmama took her breakfast in her room and never appeared in public before noon, except on Sundays, and was not present at these discussions.

'And I'll need a party frock, Mama,' said Amelia, striking while the iron was hot.

'Well,' said Mama. 'Well, if you like, you could have one instead of a birthday present.'

Amelia always got a surprise present on her birthday. She loved coming down to breakfast on her birthday morning and seeing a special package with a big bow by her place at table. For a moment Amelia wavered. She would miss that lovely sense of anticipation before she opened the present. But it was more important to her to have the new frock.

'Thank you, Mama,' she said. 'That would be a lovely present.'

And this was the reason that Amelia and Mama were on the tram, swaying through Rathmines, over the canal at Portobello, down Camden Street and Dame Street, skirting the gates of Trinity College and on past the Houses of Parliament, over the Liffey to Sackville Street and the Pillar.

The air was fresh and sweet with spring as they left Kenilworth Square, and it gradually filled with the thronging sounds of the city as they approached the river. Sackville Street itself was alive with people scurrying about their business, but none of them, Amelia was sure, were on such happy business as she and her mama.

Inside Clery's it was warm and muffled, after the noisy street. The lady shop assistants wore black skirts with deep belts and trim white blouses, and they all wore their hair neatly pinned up. Some of the more dashing ones wore neckties, like men. A gentleman with an enormous moustache and an ebony cane paced up and down, keeping an eye out for shop-lifters, pick-pockets and trouble-makers.

In the fabric department, they were served by a shop assistant with a linen measuring tape around her neck. She rolled out bolts of material with a flick of her wrist. The silks and satins and lacy materials cascaded in glorious colours over the counters. Mama fingered all the materials and shook her head. This one was too coarse and that one was too fine and the other one was too expensive.

'Ah,' she said, satisfied at last, when a pale blue glazed cotton stripe was rolled out. Amelia looked at it in horror. It was quite pretty – the sort of thing you might make a couple of light summer dresses for a small girl out of – but not what Amelia had in mind at all.

'But, Mama,' she whispered fiercely, 'I want silk – crimson silk, or cherry.'

The shop assistant looked from Amelia to Mama. 'Is it for yourself, Miss?' she asked.

Amelia nodded.

'Do you not think you should take whatever your mammy chooses?'

Amelia's face got hot and tears stung her eyelids. She said nothing.

'Oh no, no,' Mama said gamely. 'This is for a party frock. It's a birthday present. My daughter must have whatever she prefers – within reason, of course. She seems to have her heart set on crimson. Show us something suitable, if you please.'

Amelia looked up at Mama in astonishment. She had been sure her mother was going to insist on something sensible.

The shop assistant said nothing, but rolled out bolt after bolt of red fabric. There was every shade of red, in silk, satin, cotton, damask, velvet and chiffon, and now Amelia started to finger the fabrics, rubbing them between her fingers to feel the quality. Every now and then, she would pick up a length of material that had dropped over the edge of the counter and hold it up to her body and take a look in the glass. But no matter how many fabrics the shop assistant produced, there didn't seem to be one that was right. She looked pale and miserable in the mirror, and her green eyes looked dull and watery and pinkish around the rims. Amelia looked at her mother in despair. 'They don't suit me, Mama,' she said in a strangled voice.

'No, they don't,' said the shop assistant flatly. 'Someone with your colouring should wear yellow or green.'

'Well, why on earth didn't you say so earlier?' said Mama mildly.

'But you said, Madam, that the young lady was to have whatever she preferred.' The shop assistant smirked.

'Well, perhaps she will prefer what you show her next,' Mama said in an unusually severe voice.

So then the assistant brought golds and marigolds, primroses, lemons and buttery colours and then she brought bottles and jades and limes and leafy greens, some sprigged with tiny flowers, some patterned with stripes and plaids, some plain.

'That's it!' shouted Amelia in excitement, when the assistant rolled out a deep emerald silk. She snatched a handful of the cloth and pulled at it until she had several yards of it, then she wound it around her body and turned triumphantly to Mama.

Her eyes were shining, and her hair hung over her emerald shoulders like spun gold. She looked wonderful, and she knew it, even though she was only wrapped in the material. It rustled and sighed against her as only silk can, and it glowed against her skin.

Mama flinched when the shop assistant told her the price per yard, and even Amelia was shocked at how expensive it was. All the same, Mama asked the assistant to cut enough to make a dress for Amelia and to assemble whatever haberdashery items would be needed to complete it.

The assistant measured out the silk on a brass yardstick that was screwed to the counter, and cut it with a pinking shears that made a crisp sound. Then she made up a paper twist with hooks and eyes, bias binding, small pearl buttons and a spool of deep green thread, laid it on the folded fabric and made the lot into a neat brown-paper parcel tied with string. She knotted the string into a bow so that Amelia could carry it, and handed it over. Then she wrote a docket and read out the total to Mama. Mama took out her purse and counted out the amount to the nearest shilling. The shop assistant put the money and the docket into a little wooden vessel, and then she shot it off on the pneumatic money transfer system to the cash office. Presently another little wooden vessel came whizzing back, and the shop assistant unscrewed it and handed the contents to Mama – a sixpenny bit and her receipt. Mama folded up the receipt and put it in her purse, and she handed the sixpence to Amelia.

Amelia gasped. A whole sixpence! And it wasn't even her birthday, not yet. She picked up the parcel, and together they left the shop, Amelia swinging her precious package on its loop of string.

'Oh, thank you, Mama,' she said fervently when they got out on the street, and there and then she flung her arms around her mother.

Mama didn't seem a bit surprised, though it had been months since she had had a spontaneous hug from Amelia. She squeezed Amelia back and she whispered in her ear in wicked imitation of the assistant, 'But you said, Madam, that she was to have whatever she preferred.'

Amelia giggled and, extricating herself from the hug, replied in Mama's icy tones, 'Well, perhaps she'll prefer what you show her next.'

And mother and daughter held their sides and laughed

and laughed under the clock outside Clery's. People passing by smiled to see the two of them, so gay and carefree on a Wednesday afternoon in the spring sunshine.

It wasn't until she was snuggled up in bed that night and just drifting off to sleep that Amelia was struck by the illogicality of something Papa had said that morning. Only right-angled triangles had hypotenuses anyway! What could Papa have been thinking of? Had he deliberately been provoking her, because he knew she needed a good weep? Good old Papa! thought Amelia, smiling sleepily. And good old Mama! Amelia Pim really was a very lucky girl.

# At the Dressmaker's

Amelia was on her way downstairs the next day when she met a huge pile of freshly washed and ironed linen lurching up. 'Is that you, Mary Ann?' she said to the pile of linen.

'Yeff, miff,' came a muffled voice that might have been Mary Ann's and might not have been, from behind the pile of sheets.

Amelia climbed back up to the return landing. 'Gangway, Mary Ann,' she called. 'You can come on up now.'

And the pile of bedlinen swayed unsteadily up. Gradually, Mary Ann's skirt and then her black-stockinged ankles and shoes came into view under the pile of washing, and Mary Ann arrived with a sigh of relief on the half-landing.

'Here, let me help,' said Amelia, taking the top third off the bundle, to reveal Mary Ann's face, red with exertion, and her cap knocked to one side.

'Hello,' said Mary Ann with a grin, passing Amelia and continuing on around the corner and up to the main landing. Amelia followed her to the hot-press, with her smaller bundle of sheets. They were fragrant with soap and sunshine and the hot, toasty smell of the iron.

Mary Ann laid the linen lovingly on the shelves, spreading lavender bags between the layers, and then turned to take

Amelia's pile. 'Thanks, Miss,' she said. 'We keep meeting on the stairs.'

'Amelia, for heaven's sake,' said Amelia. 'How's your mother, Mary Ann?'

'Much better, Miss. Amelia, I mean. Thanks to your ma.'

'What do you mean?'

'Well, you see, the medicine wasn't doing her any good. Your ma said that was because she wasn't getting enough nourishment. She said giving medicine to a person who's not eating properly is like pouring it down the drain. So she started sending broth to my mother. And within a week, you could see the difference. She's got a bit of colour back, and I really think the medicine is doing her some good now.'

'Oh,' said Amelia. 'I didn't know.'

'She's a living saint, your ma is,' said Mary Ann.

Amelia thought this a strange thing to say. Of course, Amelia didn't go to church, but she had seen inside one or two on a few occasions, and the statues of saints she had seen were mostly very dreary-looking people with long faces who would trip up if they were alive, because their eyes were always cast heavenwards. Mama wasn't the least bit like any of them.

'And if it wasn't for her,' Mary Ann was saying, 'my ma'd be a dead saint, like all the other saints.' And she gave a laugh at her macabre little joke.

'How can you laugh about that, Mary Ann?' said Amelia in a shocked voice.

'Ah, Miss, you have to learn to laugh. It's the only thing that keeps you going, sometimes, don't you find?'

'No,' said Amelia. 'At least, I never thought about it.'

'Well, I've thought about it. And I can tell you it's the truth. A good laugh sees you through many a worrisome moment.'

'And what about your brother Patrick, Mary Ann?' Amelia asked.

'What about him?' said Mary Ann stiffly.

'Well, I mean, is he still ... is he still, you know, in prison?'

'Yes, he is, I'm proud to say,' said Mary Ann.

'Proud!' Amelia was stunned. How could anyone possibly be proud to have a prisoner in the family?

'Yes, Miss. I'm proud to be the sister of a patriot.'

'What's that?' asked Amelia. She had a vague idea it was something out of the Old Testament, but that didn't seem very appropriate.

'It means someone who puts his country before his king,' said Mary Ann staunchly.

'But the king *is* the country, isn't he? In a manner of speaking.'

'We don't see it that way. We serve neither king nor kaiser, but Ireland.'

'Gosh!' breathed Amelia, not too sure what Mary Ann was on about, but impressed by the sound of it. 'Are you a Nationalist, Mary Ann?'

'And a Socialist,' nodded Mary Ann.

'Oh dear!'

'Don't sound so disapproving, Miss Amelia. Your ma and da are Socialists too, or the next thing to it.'

'Oh no. We're Quakers.'

'That's what I mean. Friends of prisoners and champions of the poor, that's what the Quakers are, I've been told. You people are pacificists, of course, but I don't hold that against you.'

'Thank you. I'm glad.'

'You're very welcome.'

The two girls smiled at one another. Just then, Amelia's mother's voice came calling up the stairs: 'Amelia! Do get a move on! We're supposed to be there ten minutes ago.'

'Oops!' said Amelia. 'Mary Ann, I have to run. I'm being fitted for a gorgeous new dress. You'll love it!'

'Goodbye, Miss. Amelia, I mean,' said Mary Ann, but she was talking to the air, for Amelia had flown down the stairs with a clatter of feet and a whoop of laughter. Mary Ann could hear excited chattering in the hall as Amelia and her mother got their coats on. Presently the front door banged and the chattering subsided.

Mary Ann smiled to herself as she smoothed the linen down. Young Amelia had a few things to learn. Life wasn't all tram-rides to Clery's and appointments with the dressmaker. But no doubt she would find that out soon enough.

The dressmaker congratulated Amelia on her choice of fabric and she took approving notes about the style Amelia wanted and added a few suggestions of her own. Amelia and the dressmaker agreed that Amelia's birthday frock was going to be perfectly beautiful.

'Don't you think it's going to be lovely, Mama?' asked Amelia, standing on a little stool with her arms stretched out so that the dressmaker could measure her.

'Quite,' said Mama vaguely, peering out of the dressmaker's front window into the street. 'Dear, dear,' she went on, though Amelia couldn't be sure whether she was talking to herself or not, 'I do hate to see those children looking so ragged and hungry.'

'Are those Kelly children playing outside my house again?' said the dressmaker impatiently. 'I've told Mrs Kelly over and over again to keep her brats – I beg your pardon, her young'uns – out of the way of my ladies. "Ladies don't like to be troubled by your br... your childer, Mrs Kelly," I tell her. "It puts them off. It's bad for trade." Honest to God, they're no better than tinkers, those Kellys.'

'It looks to me,' said Amelia's mother, 'as if they don't get enough to eat. Is their father working?'

'No, Ma'am. Not since the lock-out. A lot of the men from these cottages worked on the trams. Most of them went back to work, of course, but not Kelly. He was too proud to sign Mr Martin Murphy's anti-union papers, so he never got taken on again. I blame that Mr Larkin and his communist ideas! Coming over here from England and stirring up trouble, it's a holy disgrace, so it is. Himself and that Countess Markievicz should be tied together and thrown off a cliff, if you ask me. We don't need their foreign ideas here, so we don't.'

Amelia looked at Mama. She didn't really understand all about the lock-out, but she knew that men had wanted to join the unions under James Larkin, and that their employers had locked them out of their work because of it. And that a lot of poor families went hungry as a result. But what Amelia was most concerned about was Mama's reaction to what the dressmaker had said about Countess Markievicz. Everyone knew about the Countess and her political activities. She was always making speeches about women's rights and about Nationalism. The Countess and Mama were not exactly friends, but they did serve on some of the same committees.

'And what about the mother?' asked Amelia's mother, not mentioning her connections with the Countess.

'A brazen hussy!'

'No, I mean, has she work?'

'She used to be in service, before she was married. Now she helps out sometimes in the house where she was employed, when they have guests in and need someone extra in the kitchen.'

'And otherwise?'

'That's all.'

'So, how do they live?'

The dressmaker had finished measuring Amelia and now she was making little marks with a piece of french chalk on the material. She shrugged in answer to Mama's question.

Mama shook her head sadly.

'How many children has Mrs Kelly?' asked Amelia, remembering what Lucinda had said about poor people.

'Five, and one on the way. Her last baby died. Just as well, otherwise there'd be seven of them soon, not counting the parents.'

'Six children!' said Amelia. 'That's too many!'

'What ever do you mean, Amelia?' asked Mama, her cheeks pink with sudden anger. 'There's no such thing as too many children. There's only not enough food to feed them.'

'But it's the same thing, Mama. If you have more children than you can feed, then you have too many.'

'No, it's *not* the same thing,' said Mama hotly. 'If you have more children than you can feed, then you are poor, that's all. Lots of our friends and relations have five or six children, and each one is precious. Do you think these people's children are any less precious to them?'

'No, Mama,' said Amelia, feeling a little ashamed of what she had said, but also feeling that there was something illogical about Mama's argument.

'Mama?' said Amelia when they had left the dressmaker's cottage and had turned onto the Harold's Cross Road, back towards home.

'Yes?'

'Nobody uses the orangery much any more, do they?'

'The orangery? Oh that conservatory place. Why, no. I don't think anyone's even been into it for years.'

'Why's that, Mama?'

'Well, I don't really know. It was your grandfather's special project, I remember. After he died, nobody bothered much with it. The roof leaked, and the furniture, which was just that light bamboo stuff, got ruined by the rain, I think. So you couldn't sit in it after that.'

'Mama, would it be a very expensive job to fix the roof?'

'No, I don't think so. Were you thinking we might use it again? That's rather a nice idea. I often think myself that it's a shame it's fallen into disuse. It would be pleasant to sit in at this time of year. We wouldn't have to replace all the furniture at once. We could use a few of the old things that are there already, and gradually we might get something more suitable.'

'I was just thinking of the roof, Mama,' said Amelia, thrilled that her plan was working out so nicely. 'If we just got the roof fixed and the glass cleaned and the floor polished, and the old furniture cleared out, of course, then, Mama, wouldn't it be a lovely place for my party? We could dance in it!'

'Well ...' said Mama, hesitating.

'We couldn't dance in the drawing room, Mama, not without taking up the rug. And the dining room would have the food in it. And the morning room's too small. But the orangery would be perfect. We could serve the food in the dining room, and leave the doors to the orangery open, and people could drift in and out. Oh, Mama, say yes, do, do!'

'Yes, Amelia, you've convinced me. I don't see why we couldn't do as you suggest. It's wasteful to have a lovely room like that and not to use it. A room so full of light. When I think about those people living in those dark little cottages with their tiny windows, hardly ever getting to see God's good sunshine at all, it makes me ashamed to be letting the orangery run to wrack and ruin.'

'Oh, Mama, thank you!' Amelia breathed, hardly able to believe it. Her very own special room for her own special party!

'We'll have a word with Mick Moriarty tomorrow and see what he can do with the roof. And ... I've just had a splendid idea, Amelia.' Amelia's mother gripped her daughter by the wrists and swung her around in a little dance on the pavement. 'We'll sell the old furniture to the rag-and-bone man when he calls on Thursday, and we'll give the proceeds to Mary Ann, to buy something for her family. She'll certainly earn it with all the extra work this party is going to make for her and Cook. Now, in addition to that, we'll need more help in the kitchen for the party. We'll get Mrs Kelly in! And that'll mean a little extra for her family. I'll go right back and ask her now!'

Amelia's mother's eyes were shining almost as much as Amelia's. It was just like her to turn a perfectly good idea for a party into a social campaign. Amelia hoped she wouldn't want to send out suffragette propaganda with the party invitations! But really she didn't mind turning back to Harold's Cross Cottages one little bit, even though her feet were tired and she was ready for her tea.

# Oranges and Lemons

Amelia often went with Mama to Findlater's shop to get the groceries. The shop was large and cool and it had a special fruity, sugary smell that Amelia loved. The manager always came out from his office behind the shop, if he heard that the Pims were there, to pay his respects. He would lean over the counter, to where the biscuit tins were ranged with their glass lids slanted outwards so that the customer could see the tempting biscuits inside, nestling on their greaseproof-paper beds, and, flipping a lid, he would take out a biscuit and hold it up ceremoniously to Amelia. He was a large plump grey-haired man with old-fashioned sideburns and a large pocket watch that Amelia used to play with when she was little. Mama and Amelia both took wicker baskets, to carry home the things they needed immediately. The rest would be delivered later in the day by cart. They didn't need to carry a purse, as they had an account at the shop, which Papa settled every month.

This day, however, Mr O'Connell didn't make an appearance when Amelia and Mama came into the shop. He must be out, thought Amelia, or else he didn't realise they were there. But the new young shopboy was very attentive. He lifted up the flap of the counter and opened the little half-door and came out to the customer's side of the counter to get a chair for Mama to sit on. Then he went back to his own side of the counter and took a pencil from behind his ear, which he licked, so that he could take down Mama's list.

Mama had a long list of requirements, and the counter was soon quite covered with food and household goods for the Pim family and servants: currants and raisins and prunes and dried apricots, sugar and salt and flour, semolina and rice and macaroni and cornflour and breadsoda, rashers of bacon and plump, damp strings of sausages, a score of eggs, washing soda and cakes of soap and a little bag of blue for whitening linen, sugar soap and borax powder for cleaning, half-a-dozen lemons, half-a-dozen oranges and a pound of bananas, cabbages, cauliflowers, onions, carrots and parsnips from the greengrocery department, and two thin white paper bags of biscuits, plain and fancy, which the shopboy weighed out carefully, adding an extra biscuit in the end, for good measure.

'Can I tempt you to a half-pound of Barry's tea, all the way from Cork?' asked the shopboy helpfully, not liking actually to suggest that Mama had forgotten something.

'Oh, I think you'll find it's come from much further afield than Cork,' said Mama waggishly. 'But no, thank you, we are Pims, the wine and tea merchants. We have our own sources of tea.'

'I'm sorry, Ma'am.' The shopboy blushed deeply. His blush clashed with his bright orange hair, so that he looked quite unattractive. Amelia felt sorry for him. She smiled at him, but he didn't notice.

'That's all right. How could you be expected to know?' said Mama kindly.

'No, it's not that, Ma'am,' said the boy. Then he leant over the counter and said something to Mama that Amelia couldn't hear.

'Oh, not at all, not at all,' said Mama brightly. 'I'm sure it's some mistake. I'll send my husband in to talk to Mr O'Connell as soon as he gets home and it'll all be settled up in no time. Now don't you feel bad about it at all. I quite understand.'

And Mama turned to leave the shop, taking Amelia by the elbow.

'But, Mama,' said Amelia, digging her heels in, 'we haven't taken the things we'll be needing immediately.'

'There's nothing that we need immediately,' said Mama firmly.

'But, Mama, the biscuits. You said we could have lemon puffs for tea. You promised, Mama.' Amelia thought she was going to cry, and she knew Edmund certainly would when he found out.

'Nonsense, Amelia,' said Mama, steering her daughter out of the shop. 'Lemon cake, I said. Cook's made a lemon cake. I'm sure she said she had.'

Amelia was suspicious. She swung her empty basket as she walked home. If Mama hadn't intended to bring some of the goods home, why had they brought their baskets, she asked herself. But she didn't say anything, just swung her basket pointedly and walked with fierce little steps.

Amelia was right. There was no lemon cake for tea that day, just bread and butter and jam – not even lemon curd. But Mama didn't offer any explanations for her fib, and Amelia knew better than to challenge her.

In any case, Amelia soon forgot all about the episode in Findlaters and the lemon puffs. She had more important things to think about. She and Mama interviewed Mick Moriarty in the back garden on the subject of the orangery roof.

Mick Moriarty took his cap off, using both hands and then replaced it on his head, even further back from his forehead than normal. This was a sign that he was thinking hard. Amelia held her breath.

'Aye,' he said at last, took the cap off again and replaced it in its normal position over his brow.

Amelia sighed with relief. That meant he thought he could fix it.

It only took him a day – that and a ladder, a football-sized lump of putty, and a few choice curses which Mama pretended not to hear. In between fixing panes in place he would throw the ball of putty down to Amelia, and she would keep it warm and pliable by pulling and rolling it in her hands, while Mick Moriarty did a bit of knife work. The putty was lovely stuff to manipulate, like elastic dough, and it smelt almost good enough to eat.

They left it for a day to harden, and then Amelia and Mary Ann went at the glass with newspapers soaked in methylated spirit. They cleaned every bit of glass as high as they could reach, and Mick Moriarty got his ladder and cleaned the roof for them.

After they had finished, Amelia and Mary Ann stood in the middle of the orangery, from which all the dusty old furniture had been cleared away, in an ankle-deep wash of medicinal-smelling newspapers and admired their sparkling glasswork. The sun obligingly came out and shone with special brilliance through the glass and onto the two girls, making their hair glint and gleam, as if to approve their work.

With a sigh of satisfaction, Amelia helped Mary Ann to pile the black and sodden newspapers into buckets and carry them through the house to the kitchen, where they poked them into the range. The fire shot up voraciously to eat the spirituous newsprint, and the girls laughed as they fed it more and more papers. Cook caught them at it and threw her hands up in despair, telling them the chimney would catch fire if they didn't look out, but they just laughed at her and stuffed the last few scrunches of newspaper into the range's black mouth.

Then they scrubbed their filthy hands at the scullery sink, and Mary Ann made tea. She used the earthenware kitchen teapot, not the silver one Amelia was used to, and the tea was hot and sweet and strong. They ate bread and dripping with it, which was the normal kitchen teatime fare. Amelia thought it was heaven to sit at the sturdy deal table and eat thick cuts of bread with Mary Ann and Cook, and not have to listen to Edmund breathing in that irritating way of his, or watch Grandmama at her eternal needlepoint and eat daintily in the drawing-room way.

'Isn't this fun, Mary Ann?' she said, even though her mouth was half-full and she should have waited till it was empty.

To Amelia it was like a picnic, but of course to Mary Ann it was nothing special, except that Amelia was there. Even so, Mary Ann said, 'Yes, Amelia.' There, she'd done it! She'd called her Amelia, without even flinching.

Amelia noticed. She didn't say anything, but she gave Mary Ann an extra-specially warm smile. And Mary Ann grinned back.

And that was how the orangery came to be a crystal dome once more, full of nothing but clear, sparkling air. By now the emerald silk dress was almost ready, Papa had secured the promise of a gramophone, and plans for the food and decorations were well under way. Amelia had a lurching feeling in her insides every time she thought about the party, but she took a deep breath and reminded Mama that it was time to write the invitations.

So they sat down one evening with Papa's best fountain pen and a pile of smooth square white cards edged with gold and wrote notes to all Amelia's classmates and her cousins Louise and Beatrice. 'And Joshua, Mama,' said Amelia.

'Joshua? Oh, I'm sure your cousin Joshua won't want to come to a girls' party.'

'But, Mama, we'll need some boys. For the dancing.'

'Ah, for the dancing,' said Mama with a knowing nod. 'I

see. I knew there must be some point to boys. Goodness knows, they're pretty useless otherwise.'

Amelia was too distracted even to notice that Mama was making a little joke. She chewed Papa's fountain pen and looked out of the window.

'And what other young men did you have in mind, Amelia? I don't suppose poor Josh is expected to do all the honours.'

'Mary Webb has a brother,' said Amelia without enthusiasm. 'And Dorothea Jacob has a cousin, a boy-cousin, I mean. Lucinda's brother is almost sixteen. Do you think that's too old, Mama?'

'I expect he's almost ready to draw a pension,' said her mother, 'but we could ask him anyway, and if he can still walk without a stick, perhaps he might be prevailed upon to come.'

'I can't think of any more,' wailed Amelia. 'Oh, Mama, have any of your suffragettes got sons?'

'Are you sure that is the sort of boy you want to mix with, Amelia?' asked her mother wickedly.

'Why, Mama! You're a suffragette.'

'And I'm all right?'

'Oh yes, Mama. Of course you are.'

'I'm pleased to hear it,' said Mama. 'Sometimes, Amelia, I think you are so disapproving of everything I do, that I almost feel guilty.'

'Oh, Mother!' said Amelia. 'It's not up to me to approve or disapprove of what you do.' But she knew, deep down inside, what her mother meant.

'No, of course it isn't. But still, one doesn't like to feel one's own daughter thinks one is crackers.'

'Mama, I don't think you're crackers. I think perhaps you're a little ... well, perhaps a little quick to get involved in things. But not crackers.'

'Ah well,' said Mama. But she didn't finish the sentence.

Just then Papa came into the room, smoking his curly pipe and scenting the air with it. He was in his carpet slippers and had on his comfortable at-home look.

'What are the ladies up to?' he asked in his gallant way.

'Writing invitations, Papa,' said Amelia. 'For the birthday party.'

'Ah, next week!' said Papa, ruffling Amelia's hair.

'Oh, and Papa, can the guests have a ride in the motor-car? I promised.'

'What?' said Papa, in mock horror. 'Do you think I'm running a motorised hackney-cab? Or a funfair ride?'

'That's right, Papa,' said Amelia, laughing up at him. 'They're all so excited at the thought.'

'Well, you tell all the young ladies to wear warm coats, and we'll see if we can't manage a spin around the square.'

It was going to be such fun, Amelia knew it. Cook was already stacking goodies in the pantry, and Edmund had helped Amelia to make paper lanterns to hang up, and streamers from coloured paper, and the orangery was looking so splendid and now Papa was going to come home early from the office and take people on motor-car rides. Amelia wasn't too sure herself how the dancing part would go, but she knew that was what the girls at school expected, so she just hoped they would know how to handle it. It was all going to be so wonderful. The best party ever.

Amelia was so busy imagining it, and breathing slowly to calm the lurching excitement in her tummy, that she didn't notice the anxious glance her mother exchanged with her father over her head.

And even if she had, she would have assumed it had something to do with Edmund, whose cold hadn't seemed to get any better. In fact, it had got worse. Amelia could hear him coughing and spluttering in the night, even though he still had a fire in his room every evening.

# The Birthday Present

Amelia woke up earlier than usual, as she always did on birthdays. She lay in bed, pretending it was just an ordinary day and forcing herself to think about dreary things like homework and lacrosse practice. Then, just as she had almost convinced herself that it was any old Tuesday, the realisation that it was really and truly her thirteenth birthday and the day of her party would come flooding back into her mind, and the excitement would make her stomach turn right over so that she groaned into her pillow.

When she heard Mary Ann rattling around downstairs, cleaning the grates, Amelia knew it was time to get up, so she slipped out of bed and washed hurriedly, pouring water from the big flower-patterned ewer into the basin and soaping herself quickly and then rinsing and patting herself dry. She brushed her teeth in the last of the water, struggled into her everyday school clothes and her heavy school boots and, pulling the hairbrush quickly through her smooth hair, she left the bedroom and flew downstairs.

Breakfast was laid since the night before, and Amelia could hear Mary Ann's footsteps coming from the kitchen, but none of the family had made an appearance yet. She paced to the window and looked out onto the garden, which was fresh with a recent shower of spring rain and bright with daffodils. She didn't know whether she wished the others would appear, or whether she wanted to eke out the anticipation a little longer.

The door opened quietly, and in came Mary Ann, carrying a breakfast tray.

'Happy birthday, Amelia,' she said with a grin. She put the breakfast tray down, and came over to Amelia at the window. She pushed a small package into Amelia's hand, and then scuttled out the door.

Amelia certainly hadn't expected Mary Ann to give her a birthday present. She opened the flat little package with shaking fingers. Inside was a plain white handkerchief, the kind you could buy very cheaply in any of the big shops in town. Amelia knew that Mary Ann couldn't spare even a penny or two to be buying handkerchiefs for a girl like Amelia, who was so much better off.

She shook the handkerchief out, and the fresh smell of new cotton rose up to meet her. Just then, Amelia noticed a little sprig of embroidery in the corner. It was the letters AP intertwined, with a circle of lily-of-the-valley around them, all done in tiny stitches in cream thread. The stitching was so neat and smooth and the colour so discreet that Amelia had almost missed it. This was Mary Ann's real present – her own handiwork. Amelia was very touched, and she hadn't even had a chance to say thank you.

Edmund was the next to come bursting through the door. He had a package in his hand too. 'Happy birthday, Mealy,' he said, calling her by his baby-name for her. His present was a toy train carriage, gaily painted in royal blue with bright red and gold trimmings – just the sort of thing Edmund loved himself. Its very inappropriateness made Amelia smile, and she leant over and kissed her little brother and said 'Thank you, Edmund' in the sweetest voice she could manage.

She led Edmund by the hand to the breakfast table, where

Mary Ann had set tea and coffee and warm muffins and apricot jam. As she sat down, Amelia noticed yet another package, wrapped in blue tissue paper and done up with a narrow pink ribbon, by her plate.

This was a puzzle. She'd already got Edmund's present. Mama and Papa were giving her the silk party dress. And Grandmama always gave Amelia a crisp and sweet-smelling ten-shilling note for her birthday, which Papa whipped away immediately to lodge to Amelia's bank account. So where could this have come from?

Mama and Papa appeared together, just as Amelia was turning the little packet over. It was lumpy and heavy. 'Happy birthday, darling!' they said together, kissing and hugging their daughter. When they'd sat down, Amelia opened the little blue packet. It contained the loveliest gold watch on a golden chain that Amelia had ever seen. She slipped it over her head and turned the wrapping paper inside out, looking for a card or note to see where that lovely present could have come from.

But there was no card. Amelia looked up enquiringly at Mama, who looked blankly back at her. Then she looked at Papa, whose eyes were looking extra blue, for no reason at all. 'Was it you, Papa?' she whispered.

'Might have been,' said Papa, pretending to be very interested in the toast rack, all of a sudden.

'Oh, Papa!' exclaimed Amelia, running to hug her father again.

'Charles!' said Mama, in an alarmed voice. 'Charles, you know we can't ...'

Amelia was amazed by her mother's tone. She turned to look at her. 'Is something wrong, Mama?' she asked.

'No, Amelia. Nothing. I'm just surprised, that's all. I didn't realise Papa had bought the watch.' And she smiled at her daughter.

But Amelia felt uneasy all the same. This exchange between her parents reminded her of something, but she couldn't think what.

'Thank you, Papa,' she said quietly. 'But you know it was extravagant. You've already got me the lovely new dress, and you're giving the party.'

'Dress! Party! That's all very well,' cried Papa. 'But I couldn't bear to think of my little princess with nothing to open on her birthday morning. Now, let's all drink a birthday toast to Amelia.'

'In coffee, Charles?' said Mama.

'Tea, coffee, milk ... who cares? Here's to Amelia. May this be your happiest birthday ever. And many happy returns of the day.'

'Happy birthday, Amelia,' said Mama with a smile, raising her coffee-cup.

Papa leant over and clinked his coffee-cup against Amelia's, and Edmund, overcome with the excitement, started to sing 'Happy birthday to you!' in his hoarse, wheezy voice.

Amelia beamed on them all, and she felt just like a real princess, as she fingered her delicate gold chain and felt the weight of the gold watch, which was nestling against the front of her dress. She raised her cup regally and tried to say 'Thank you all,' but only a squeaking sound came out. She was so happy, she couldn't speak.

People with birthdays got off lightly at school. The teachers made a point of not asking them their lessons, so the morning passed pleasantly enough. The girls told each teacher in turn that they were all invited to Amelia's party, and each teacher gallantly agreed to excuse them all from homework. The girls cheered as the teachers capitulated in turn to their request, and every time they did it, Amelia felt a glow inside. It was all because of her that everyone was so jolly.

At lunchtime, in the school yard, the girls made a dash for Amelia. Two of them grabbed her under the armpits, and another two got hold of her ankles, and they heaved her from side to side, with her pinafore trailing on the ground. Amelia was laughing so much she couldn't even yell at them to stop. Then they dropped her onto her bottom on the ground, thirteen times, once for every year, calling out the numbers and bumping her faster and faster as they approached thirteen. They were careful not to hurt her, but the final bump was quite a jolt all the same, as the girls let her go abruptly and then collapsed in a giggling heap on top of her. Amelia got a mouthful of Dorothea Jacob's hair and Mary Webb's elbow poked her in the eye.

Gradually the squirming mass of boots, pinafores and bodies disentangled itself, and Amelia sat up and combed her fingers through her hair in case there were any twigs or leaves in it. 'This is the Grosvenor Academy for Young Ladies, I'll have you know,' she said, brushing herself down, 'not the Grosvenor Academy for Young Ponies.'

Suddenly, a dreadful thought occurred to her. She missed the little tug of the heavy watch. She reached around her neck to feel for the chain. There was nothing there! Amelia first went very red, then she went very pale and silent, and finally she burst into tears. She rolled over onto her stomach, heaved herself onto all fours, and went crawling around the school yard, frantically pawing the ground and shouting, between sobs, 'My watch. My new gold watch!'

When the others realised what had happened, they too started to search everywhere for the gold watch that they'd all admired so much earlier in the day. But it was nowhere to be found.

'It's bound to turn up, Amelia,' Lucinda said comfortingly. 'Are you sure it hasn't wriggled its way down your front and got tangled up in your petticoat?'

'Of course it hasn't,' said Amelia crossly. 'I'd feel a heavy thing like a watch if it was caught in my clothes. Oh dear, oh dear! What'll I tell Papa?' And she burst into tears all over again.

'Will he be very vexed, Amelia?' asked Lucinda, with a shake in her voice.

'No, no. He's never angry with me, never. But even so, I can't bear to tell him I've lost his special present to me. Oh Lucy! What am I going to do?'

The others had drifted away by now, and Amelia and Lucinda were left alone in the school yard, their teeth chattering in the early spring wind, their faces looking pinched and cold. But they were shivering with disappointment and upset as much as with the cold of the afternoon.

'Never mind,' said Lucinda at last, putting her arm around her friend's shoulder. 'You'd better just try to put it out of your mind for the moment and enjoy the party this afternoon. Tomorrow, when all the excitement is over, we'll think some more about the watch, and see if we can't come up with a plan.'

'All right,' said Amelia heavily. 'We'd better get back to class anyway. The second bell has already rung.'

All through afternoon school, Amelia thought and thought about the watch. First she tried to think what might have happened to it, where she might have dropped it. And then, when her head ached from thinking about that, she thought about how she was going to break the news to Mama and Papa. She found it very hard to take Lucinda's advice and just forget about it for the moment.

When the bell rang for the end of school, the girls all crowded around Amelia again. They'd all forgotten about the watch, and were full of excited chatter about the party. They plagued Amelia with questions, about who was coming, what there would be to eat, whether there would be dancing, whether the mamas were to come too. Amelia tried to smile and answer their questions patiently, but all she wanted was to get home to her own bedroom, and have a good weep. All the lovely birthday feeling had drained away and Amelia almost wished there wasn't going to be a party later that afternoon. She just didn't see how she was going to face it.

# The Party

Amelia dragged herself wearily home, wishing vainly all the way that she'd never got the wretched watch in the first place, that she'd been more careful with it, that there wasn't going to be a stupid party that afternoon, that she was still twelve, that birthdays, parties and watches had all never been invented. But as soon as she entered the house, she got whisked away on a magic carpet of excited anticipation that seemed to be swooping around and carrying the whole household with it.

The first person she met was Mary Ann, laden down with the most enormous trayful of hors d'oeuvres that Amelia had ever seen. She was manoeuvring the tray in front of her, as if it were a particularly unwieldy bicycle with a large front basket, like the one the butcher's boy used for deliveries, with her elbows sticking out even more pointedly than normal. Her cap was slipping down her shiny forehead onto her pointy nose, and she kept jerking her head back to try and jolt the cap into position, because she didn't have a free hand to adjust it.

Amelia stood hesitantly in the hallway. She was a bit daunted by the size of the tray, so instead of taking it she said, 'Hold still a minute, Mary Ann,' and she reached up and fixed Mary Ann's errant cap.

'Thanks,' said Mary Ann with a sniffle. 'Lawny, I'm run off my feet. I suppose you couldn't blow my nose for me too, could you?'

'Oh no!' said Amelia, with distaste.

'Idiot!' said Mary Ann, with a high-pitched laugh. 'I was only pulling your leg.' And she turned to go into the dining room, still bearing the tray awkwardly in front of her.

'Hey, wait a minute!' said Amelia, trailing after her. 'Aren't you going to let me say thank you?'

'What?' said Mary Ann distractedly, from the doorway, turning her head to look back at Amelia.

'For the handkerchief. It's lovely. The embroidery is beautiful. Thanks, Mary Ann.'

'It's nothing,' Mary Ann mumbled and proceeded into the dining room with the tray. She preferred pulling people's legs to making polite conversation.

'How come everyone's so busy?' asked Amelia, following Mary Ann into the dining room. She could hear doors banging and feet clip-clopping along with hurried steps. And there was Mama, standing on tiptoe on a step-ladder, pinning paper chains to the picture rail.

'For goodness' sake!' said Mama, looking down at Amelia and answering the question she had put to Mary Ann. 'In case you didn't realise it, we are giving a party for twenty people in an hour's time. Really, Amelia, do you think these things just happen by themselves?'

'Of course I know they don't, but it's cold food. And there's Mrs Kelly to help in the kitchen.'

'She never showed up,' said Mary Ann, taking Amelia by the waist and bodily moving her out of the middle of the room, where she was quite in the way.

'Oh dear!' said Amelia. 'So it's just you and Cook.'

'That's right,' said Mary Ann cheerfully. 'And now if you don't mind, Miss, I've got to get back to the kitchen.'

Amelia stood for a while and wondered why Mrs Kelly hadn't shown up. Perhaps the dressmaker's assessment had been right, and the Kellys were a feckless family after all. It didn't seem to make any sense to turn down a chance to make a little extra if money was short.

As she stood and wondered, Amelia gradually noticed the transformation that had taken place in the dining room. The french doors to the orangery were open, as she had planned, so it all looked like one generous, sunlit room. Little straight rainbows, like living icicles of light, danced on the floor, as the sunshine refracted through the orangery and fell into the room. The paper lanterns Amelia and Edmund had made for the party were strung in the orangery, and Mama had even found, not real orange trees, but a few parlour palms and aspidistras to give the flavour of a proper conservatory. Through the french doors, flung open to the orangery, through the clear air of the orangery itself, and on through its crystal walls you could see the garden, all awash with spring, the fruit trees dainty in their blossomy dresses and the garden bench at the foot of the garden strewn with fallen petals.

'Oh, Mama!' breathed Amelia, completely forgetting that Mary Ann was footsore and overworked, that Mrs Kelly was feckless and foolish and that she, Amelia Pim, had lost her first ever gold watch on the very day it was given to her by her dear Papa. 'Isn't it wonderful?'

'Glad – you – like – it – darling,' said Mama with an effort. She had her arms over her head, trying to pin the edge of a paper chain to the cornice.

'I'll see if I can find something to do in the kitchen,' said Amelia, and she clattered off in that direction.

Cook, who was, as all cooks should be, a large, puddingy sort of person, whose full, soft cheeks shook when she spoke, like a half-cooked cake mixture that's still wobbly under the skewer, and who was normally, as all large, puddingy persons are, an oasis of calm and a rock of sense, was pink and flustered in the cheeks and concerned across the eyebrows. She raised one of her concerned eyebrows at Amelia as she entered the kitchen and said, 'I hope you haven't come looking for a snack, because I haven't time to get you one.' And with that, Cook ran, or at least she lurched quickly, which is the nearest that large, puddingy persons come to running, into the pantry and emerged shortly with a platter of iced buns with shiny little glacé cherries on top, for all the world like tiny casseroles with wee bright lid-knobs.

'Oh no, Cook, I've come to see if I can help.'

Cook looked mollified. She shoved the plate of iced cakes at Amelia and said, 'Well, you can take these to the dining room, but they're for after the savouries, so make sure they go on the sideboard, not the main table. You can put them next to the jellies and the trifles.'

In her delight with the orangery and the light filling the normally rather dusky dining room, Amelia hadn't even noticed the food. Now, clearing a place on the sideboard with her elbow to put the large plate of iced cakes down, she took in the splendid array of food for the first time. There were jellies, as Cook had mentioned, in three colours – green, purple and red – all beautifully turned out of their complicated moulds and glowing like translucent eastern buildings with turrets and minarets, and there were trifles in cut-glass bowls, thick with custard and studded with fruit, there were little bon-bon dishes of liquorice all-sorts, all bright and spanking, and there was, right in the centre of the desserts, a birthday cake such as Amelia had never seen before, with perfectly smooth white icing and little pink sugar roses around each of the thirteen candles. In addition, there was a spread of savouries on the large oval dining table –

olives and pickled onions, tiny sausages, anchovy toast, miniature egg-and-bacon tarts, and dainty little triangular sandwiches with the crusts cut off, with little bouquets of parsley dotted here and there among them. It was just as well Grandmama had taken Papa's advice and absented herself to Bray for the day, for she would never have stood for sandwiches with the crusts cut off.

For the next while Amelia joined in the household dither, making little journeys up from the kitchen to the dining room, sometimes meeting Mary Ann on the way, stopping occasionally to hold the step-ladder for Mama when she was at a particularly awkward bit, and even carrying extra coal to the drawing room, where any mamas who came would be entertained.

There was so much to be done, and such an air of determined excitement about it all, and Amelia was bustling so hard with the rest of them that she almost forgot to go and get ready. Mama called to her at last: 'Amelia, do you realise what time it is? They'll be here in half-an-hour. What's the point in having a watch if you don't use it to keep an eye on the time?'

A cold shiver ran over Amelia's skin, as if someone had suddenly opened a door from a warm room to a very cold outdoors and let in a wintry blast of air. She hadn't given the watch a thought for a good half-hour at least. Oh bother Mama! Why did she have to spoil everything?

'Very well, Mama,' said Amelia in a subdued voice. 'I'll go and change.'

But when she arrived in her bedroom and saw the beautiful emerald silk dress glowing on the quilt where Mama must have laid it while she was at school, Amelia's heart gave a little leap. When Amelia had last seen it, the dress had still been held together with pins, its glorious colour undimmed, but looking rather shapeless and temporary. Now it was a real ball-gown, shapely and lovely. It worked a magic spell on Amelia, and all thoughts of the lost watch slipped out of her mind again.

She fingered the silk, and it whispered to her. She picked the dress up and held it to her, and it whispered some more. She caught a handful of the stuff and did a twirl, holding the skirt out, and it shimmered as it rustled, and then it sighed and flowed as she came to a standstill and dropped her handful of material. It was like something that was alive. It was certainly something to treasure.

Amelia laid the dress reverently back on the bed and went and propped the swinging mirror on her tallboy forward and examined her face. It was just as well she did, because there was a big black coaly smudge right in the middle of her nose. Amelia dabbed at it with her sponge until she had got rid of every trace of coal dust, and then she scrubbed her nails and, with long, careful strokes, she brushed her hair, which Mama had washed the night before and dried in front of the drawing-room fire.

Finally, she stepped out of her school clothes, drew on her best stockings and slipped the emerald dress over her head, listening to its murmurings as it slid over her ears and settled on her body. She did up all the little buttons carefully, adjusted the dress in the mirror, bent down and slipped into her party pumps, and behold, Amelia Pim, age thirteen, with a pretty little nose and sea-green eyes that more or less compensated for her sticky-out ears, and a burnished waterfall of yellow hair down her back, was ready to face the world, or at least to face twenty young people of mixed sex and respectable background in search of a few hours' entertainment.

She glided down the stairs in the emerald dress, feeling as if she was floating on a silken cloud, as the dress gently billowed around her and rose up against her hands, with which she constantly smoothed and settled it. Just as she was halfway down, the doorbell rang and Mary Ann came at a gallop from the dining room with the step-ladder under her arm and made frantic signals to Amelia to open the door herself while Mary Ann made good her escape to the kitchen with the evidence. Amelia hesitated, her heart thumping, and then she gathered up her courage and opened the door. There stood Lucinda and her elder brother, her first party guests.

How could Amelia ever have thought of not inviting Lucinda's brother? That would have been a great mistake! He was tall, as sixteen-year-olds tend to be, much taller than either of the girls, and he had the same head of bubbly auburn curls that Lucinda had, except that his, cut shorter, looked less as if they were about to take over the world. He looked down at Amelia from a pair of tawny eyes, bright and devilish as his sister's, and, with a slight forward inclination of the top half of his body that might or might not have been a bow, said: 'Amelia Pim? I am Frederick Goodbody. Perhaps you remember me?'

Amelia wasn't sure if he was poking fun at her, but she thought it better to reply graciously. Just as she was about to open her mouth, she heard a muffled giggle behind her, and she knew Mary Ann must be there. She had been handling the situation nicely until she realised she was being observed, but now she could feel herself blushing. 'Hello,' she said, unceremoniously, and didn't offer to shake hands. 'Come in.' And then she immediately started to chatter nervously to Lucinda, and to fuss with the coats, ignoring Frederick, who stood gallantly by and examined Papa's hunting prints in the hallway.

Then the doorbell rang again. It was Dorothea Jacob, with her older sister and her cousin Richard. Dorothea looked a bit strange. Her face was pale, but her eyes were pink and there were two bright red spots on her cheekbones. Amelia couldn't remember inviting Elizabeth, Dorothea's sister, but she took her cape just the same and smiled at her. And before Amelia could hang up the coats, there was another ring at the door. Amelia whooshed the first guests into the dining room and turned to admit the next group, and before five minutes had passed, the party had started to happen, all by itself, without Amelia having to give it another thought.

She was a hostess.

# How the Party Ended

W hat about this famous motor-car of your papa's, Amelia?' asked Mary Webb. 'You promised us all a spin. It was going to be the star attraction of the party.' Mary's tone wasn't entirely friendly, though she tried to pretend otherwise by giving a large, moony smile as she spoke.

Everyone was puffed and pink by now, having danced to Papa's friend's gramophone for a good half-hour in a fairly confined space, which meant a certain amount of gigglesome jostling and a good deal of body heat, so that the air was over-warm and unhealthy with the scent of talcum and cheap cologne and the inside panes of the orangery were clouded. The food had all been scoffed long ago, and there was nothing left but little blobs of jelly, a few streaks of grease on the sausage plates, a quantity of crumbs and half the birthday cake, which Amelia had insisted on saving for Papa and for Edmund, who had been sent to a friend's house to keep him out of harm's way.

'Yes, Amelia,' said Lucinda, fanning herself with a napkin. 'What time do you expect your father home?'

Everyone was growing tired and restless, and they were all looking for some new diversion.

Amelia hadn't given Papa and the car a thought all afternoon. She'd been far too busy arranging to be in the right place every time Mama changed the record on the gramophone, so that Frederick Goodbody would have every chance of asking her to dance, which he did, several times.

Now she turned an anxious face to Mama. 'Is Papa late?' she asked.

'Are you not wearing your watch, Amelia, or is it just that you haven't got used to having it yet?' asked Mama.

Dorothea Jacob, who had been looking remarkably glum and pale all afternoon, even when she was dancing with Frederick, chose this moment to keel over in a faint, right in the middle of the floor. Everyone crowded around her, asking what was the matter, except Dorothea's elder sister, Elizabeth, who looked gravely the other way, as if she had never heard of Dorothea.

'Now then, now then,' said Amelia's mama, gently elbowing her way through the twittering crowd, 'stand back and let her get some air. She's probably just a bit over-excited. I have to say I did think you were all a little young for this sort of party.' And she quickly loosened the top buttons of Dorothea's blouse and pressed a glass of water to her lips.

Amelia thought she would use the diversion created by Dorothea to go and see if there was any sign of Papa.

She slipped into the drawing room, where the fire was burning brightly, talking to itself in a cheerful tone of voice, and she peered through the front window, from which she had a good view of their side of the square. It was growing dusk, so it must be time Papa came home. At this time of year he was always back well before dark. A couple of old ladies in black were taking their evening walk, tottering slowly under the overhanging trees of the square, a boy was bowling a hoop along the pavement, and a stout gentleman in a top hat trotted by on a bay mare. But there was no sign of a motor-car, and no matter how Amelia strained her ears, she could hear nothing but the rhythmic trip-trap of the stout man's mare and the whoops of the boy as he pursued his hoop.

Just as she was about to turn away, Amelia caught sight of a bent figure rounding the corner. She peered again, narrowing her eyes to be sure. Yes, it was Papa. But where was the car? Had it broken down? Often it took a lot of wheezing and effort and cranking with the starting handle to get it going in the mornings, but it had never actually broken down before.

If the car had broken down, surely Papa would have taken a cab? He wouldn't have waited for the tram, as he would be in a hurry to get home because of the party. Unless, of course, the car had broken down when he was almost home, and it wasn't worth his while to hail a cab. That must be it.

Amelia's heart lifted when she saw Papa, as it always did, even though she was disappointed that the car had broken down and she wouldn't be able to show it off to her friends. Papa must be disappointed too. He loved that car like a baby. He was for ever polishing it. Poor Papa, he did look downcast, Amelia thought. She ran from the room, through the hall, out the front door and down the steps, to meet him.

Papa didn't look up. He didn't hear her coming, though she was flying along the pavement and her feet were making a pit-pattering sound as she ran. 'Papa!' she called as she came close to him, for he was in danger of walking right past her. 'Papa!' She was almost within touching distance of him now. At last he raised his head, and Amelia saw that there were tears streaming down his cheeks.

She had never seen him weep before, not even when Clip and Clop were sold and everyone else in the family had been in mourning for days and had gone around the house with their handkerchiefs constantly at the ready, scrunched up in their hands.

Amelia stopped in her tracks. 'Oh, Papa!' she said. She didn't ask what was wrong. It couldn't be simply that the car had broken down. Perhaps Papa'd had an accident. Perhaps the car was badly damaged. Perhaps he'd knocked someone down. Oh dear! Dreadful thoughts flew around Amelia's head so fast they seemed to bump into each other and trip each other up.

Papa didn't look surprised to see Amelia standing in front of him. In fact he looked almost as if he had expected her to come and greet him, as if he had relied on her to be the one to comfort him. At exactly the same moment, father and daughter opened their arms, then they each took a step forward, and in a wink they were hugging hard on the pavement. Amelia could feel Papa's soundless sobs as he hugged her, and a tear trickled down the back of her neck. Neither of them noticed the two old ladies in black looking archly at each other as they went by on the opposite pavement. It wasn't quite the thing for papas to hug their daughters on the street, not unless it was at a railway station.

When they drew apart, Amelia slipped her hand into his and slowly they walked back to the house, hand in hand, as they used to do when Amelia was a little girl. Papa's tears had stopped now, and he managed a watery smile. 'You look lovely, princess,' he whispered. Amelia looked down at herself, in her party dress. She'd forgotten all about it.

'Oh, Papa, I lost my watch!' Amelia blurted out. Papa sighed, but he didn't scold her. Instead he said gently, 'Your watch. Good heavens, Amelia, it's nothing to lose a watch. Anyone could lose a watch. People do it all the time. I, on the other hand, have lost a fortune.'

Amelia bit her lower lip, concentrating on trying not to cry. She didn't want to make Papa feel worse. Then she said, 'You mean you've lost the car, Papa?' She knew cars were expensive. She'd heard someone say they cost a fortune. But she couldn't really imagine how anyone could lose one. Surely even if you forgot where you'd left it, you'd remember eventually.

'Not just the car, Amelia. Everything.'

Amelia didn't know what he meant. She could see his pocket watch on its chain, for example. That wasn't lost anyway. How could anyone lose everything? It didn't make sense. But she didn't ask any more questions. She knew Papa was too upset to explain.

Mama was standing in the doorway, with her most worried look on, and her hair coming down and hanging in untidy hanks around her face. Normally it irritated Amelia immensely the way Mama pinned up her hair so carelessly that it fell down at the slightest provocation, and today it was even more untidy than normal, because Mama had been exerting herself all afternoon, pinning up the paper chains and then winding up the gramophone. But on this occasion, Amelia was oddly touched by Mama's very dishevelment. It made her want to take care of Mama.

But Mama looked right over Amelia's head and into Papa's eyes. 'Oh, Charles,' she whispered when she saw his face.

'I'm sorry, Roberta, I'm so sorry.'

Amelia looked from one to the other and wondered what was going on. At last she said to Mama: 'Is Dorothea all right?'

'Dorothea?' Mama asked wonderingly, as if Amelia had enquired as to the welfare of someone on another planet.

'The red-haired girl who fainted,' explained Amelia.

'Red-haired,' repeated Mama. 'Fainted,' she said in a far-away voice.

Now Papa was patting the back of Mama's hand and steering her towards the drawing room. They had evidently forgotten not only all about Dorothea, but about the birthday party, and even, apparently, about Amelia.

Amelia felt dreadful. She was worried and upset about

Papa and whatever it was that was wrong with him, but she was exasperated that Mama had suddenly withdrawn her attention from the party and from herself, and she felt left all alone, with the responsibility for all twenty guests on her shoulders. How was she going to go back into the dining room and explain to them all that there were to be no jaunts in the new car, that, as far as she could ascertain, there was no new car? No. She couldn't do it, she thought, as she watched the drawing-room door close on her parents. She sank onto the bottom step of the staircase and buried her head in her knees, not crying, but simply looking at the dark and wishing everyone would go away and this dreadful birthday would end.

And there Mary Ann found her a few moments later. Mary Ann looked down at Amelia's curved back, the emerald silk dress stretched across the shoulder blades, and she remembered herself sitting in just that position some weeks ago. She remembered that Amelia had comforted her, and she thought that though she was only a serving girl, perhaps she could offer some comfort now in her turn.

'What's the matter, pet?' she said, using the term of affection she always used with her younger brothers and sisters.

Amelia looked up, dazed, and registered the form of the maid-of-all-work, gawky and tall above her in her black-and-white uniform and her cap tilting off to the side. 'I'm not sure,' she replied. 'But I think it's pretty dreadful.'

'Shove up a bit,' said Mary Ann, and nestled herself in between Amelia and the newel post. 'Now, what can be so dreadful? Your friend is grand. She's down in the kitchen with Cook, having a cup of nice strong tea with lots of sugar, for the shock. And your party has been a great success.'

'Oh no, it hasn't,' said Amelia, 'not an unmixed success at any rate. Papa has lost the car.'

'Lost the car?' said Mary Ann, who evidently thought this was as odd a thing as Amelia had thought it. 'Ah sure, it'll turn up.'

This reminded Amelia of what Lucinda had said about the lost gold watch, and suddenly that loss, which only hours before had seemed dreadfully distressing, now seemed distant and irrelevant, like some childish incident of long ago. To her surprise, Amelia found herself wishing that Grandmama was at home. Grandmama was severe and exacting, but she was also kind and comfortable, and Amelia wanted her to be there.

'But you see, the thing is,' Amelia went on, 'the girls were all expecting Papa to take them for a spin in the car. They have all been admiring it, because it's such a beautiful car, and they've been looking forward to getting a go in it, and they've been asking me when he was coming home. I just don't want to go in and explain.' And though she was determined not to cry, Amelia's mouth was turning down dangerously far at the corners and there was a tremble in her voice.

'I'll tell you what, Amelia,' said Mary Ann. 'You slip upstairs to your room, and I'll go in and tell them all that you're unwell, and that your daddy has been delayed, and that the party is over.'

'Oh, would you, Mary Ann?' said Amelia, her heart flooding with gratitude. She had begun to feel so weary but now she felt she had at least enough energy to climb the stairs and get into bed and put the covers over her head.

'Indeed and I will. I'll clear the place in five minutes, wait till you see, and I'll be up to you with a nice cup of tea as soon as I've got rid of them all.'

So Amelia plodded back up the stairs she had so recently floated down, patting her new dress and feeling like a fairytale princess. Now she felt like a very ordinary and very young thirteen-year-old in a dress that was about two years too old for her.

When she reached her bedroom, she finally allowed the hot tears, of disappointment, anxiety and loneliness, to come coursing down her cheeks, and she never saw how bravely Mary Ann sailed into the buzzing maelstrom of the disintegrating remains of the party and dealt with the rude assault of questions and sharp retorts the assembled young people greeted her with. She never heard either the haughty remarks they threw at each other as they jostled for their coats in the hall, and the insulting things they said about her, her family and her party as they left. Which was just as well, as she was in no fit state to face them.

# BOOK II

# Coming Down in the World

Amelia hated the new house. It was a mean little house, dark and poky, with no garden, only a yard with an outside wc, a coal bunker and a lean-to shed with no door that was useless even for storing things in because everything got wet when the wind came from the west, which it often did. And at the front there was no garden either: the hall-door opened directly onto the pavement. Amelia was mortified the way people could see right into your hall every time you came in or out your own front door, and she had perfected a method of squeezing through the tiniest opening between the door and the jamb so that the house didn't have to be thrown open to the neighbours.

Even Edmund, who was too young to bother much with his surroundings and lived most of the time in an imaginary train, noticed how mean and poky the house was. 'Where's the nursery?' he asked in a puzzled voice. 'There's a nursery at home,' he said, standing defiantly in the doorway of his tiny bedroom.

'This is home now, Edmund dear,' said Grandmama in a cheerful tone. At least, it sounded as if she meant it to be cheerful, but everyone knew she didn't really feel cheerful at all.

'No,' said Edmund. 'This isn't home. Home has a garden

and a nursery and lots of grown-up rooms and 'Melia's norngery. This place is nasty. Where's 'Melia's norngery gone?'

'Now, Edmund,' Grandmama began, and this time her voice sounded firm and patient, not pretend-cheerful any more, 'we can't live in our old house any more. You know that. We live here now. And we're very lucky to have a roof over our heads at all.'

Of course it was true that they were luckier than some people. But they didn't know any people who didn't have a roof over their heads. They only knew people who lived in large houses and had lovely things, so it was hard to believe in this luck Grandmama spoke about.

'Are we, Grandmama?' asked Edmund, looking up at the old lady. 'Why?'

'Because we're poor now, Edmund.'

'Oh,' said Edmund, considering this idea. Then he asked again: 'Why, Grandmama?'

'Because ...' Grandmama was stumped.

'Because ...' she tried again.

'Because,' she said with some conviction at last, 'we've been unfortunate.' She pronounced the last word very slowly and deliberately.

'Oh,' said Edmund again. He shrugged his little shoulders and went into his room and shut the door. He didn't really know what 'unfortunate' meant, but he knew when a grown-up had got the better of him. After a moment he opened his door and stuck his head out and called out: 'I still want to go *home*!'

But of course they couldn't go home, not now, not after what had happened. The Elders of the Meeting had come to the house in Kenilworth Square the evening after Amelia's birthday and there had been long, grave discussions in the drawing room from which Papa emerged at intervals looking very pale and with black smudges under his eyes. Mama sometimes sat in on the discussions, and sometimes she came out and sat with the children and Grandmama in the morning room.

It transpired that Papa had been forced to declare himself bankrupt. That was what he meant when he said he had lost everything. In the old days, Mama explained, the Society of Friends took a very poor view of bankruptcy, and people who went bankrupt might even be disowned by the Society.

'But it's no disgrace to be bankrupt nowadays,' Mama said firmly. 'And it doesn't mean that your father has done anything dishonest or wrong or illegal. It just means that things have gone badly in his business.'

But Amelia knew it was a disgrace all the same. Being declared bankrupt was a very dreadful thing. It meant you had failed badly at your business, and let down all your employees and the people who had lent you money or given you credit.

'In fact, we're very lucky to be Quakers,' Mama remarked. 'The Friends are doing their best to help us.'

Amelia didn't feel lucky to be a Quaker. She still hated going to Meeting, and she didn't agree with Grandmama's old-fashioned Quakerly views about 'showiness' and expensive living. But she grudgingly acknowledged that Mama had a point. At least the Friends would rally round, now they were in trouble.

Mama had gone on to say that the bailiffs would want to seize the family's goods in order to meet Papa's debts.

'Oh!' Amelia had cried. 'Is that what happened to the motor-car?'

'Yes, Amelia,' Mama had agreed. 'They took that first, because it is worth good money and is not really a necessity.'

Poor Papa, Amelia thought, and hated them for taking away the thing he loved best. They might have left it. It was mean to take it. Surely they could have taken something else!

But there was worse to come. Mama went on to explain in a low voice that the bailiffs would want to seize the house and furniture, if the debts weren't paid. Amelia gasped. But, Mama went on, her tone steady and even, they would give the family time to find somewhere new to live and wouldn't take the things they needed for day-to-day living – at least not yet.

'But ...' Amelia was horrified. She couldn't finish her sentence. She put out a hand and stroked the morning-room curtains, as if they were beloved pets that somebody was going to take away from her. She looked at the familiar furniture she had grown up with, and she felt about the chairs and tables and sideboards and cabinets almost as if they were living things that she couldn't bear to be parted from.

But there was no help for it. The house and furniture would have to be sold as quickly as possible, to get money to pay the people Papa owed – and all because Papa had made a few unwise investments. There was something about a ship being lost at sea, too, which Amelia could understand a bit, because of reading *The Merchant of Venice* at school.

'If only that wretched ship hadn't gone down!' Papa declared daily. 'There were enough goods on that boat to redeem all my debts and still leave enough to invest in the next shipload.'

Mama always sighed when he said this. She said there was no point in crying over spilt milk. Papa would argue with her then. Every day, the value of the goods on the famous ship seemed to get greater. Before long, Papa was saying that there were enough goods on that boat to keep them all in comfort for the rest of their lives.

'No, Charles, you know that's just not so,' Mama persisted, trying to reason with him. 'It was unfortunate that the ship went down, but you know in your heart that even if she had come to harbour, it would only have staved off the evil day. In another month there would have been more, bigger debts. It would take a good deal more than a single shipload to sort out our problems.'

But Papa got angry with her when she said this sort of thing.

'Really, Roberta,' Amelia overheard him say one day, 'you don't know what you're talking about, my dear. But how could you? What do you know about business?'

Amelia couldn't hear Mama's murmured reply, but Papa's riposte came loud and clear: 'Nonsense! That ship would have been the making of us. Oh, Roberta, I counted on it. I counted on it. It would have been, I tell you, it would have been the making of the business. I would have been a wealthy man, Roberta. I would, I would ... oh, oh!'

And then came some heartbreaking sounds, as if Papa were – surely he couldn't be – sobbing.

Amelia wanted to believe Papa, that it had all been just a piece of rotten luck. But try as she would to take Papa's side in these arguments, she had to admit that what Mama said seemed to make more sense. Still, that didn't make it any easier for poor Papa, living in this poky little house that the Friends had found for the family at a low rent, and plodding off to work every day to the miserable, lowly little job in a Quaker firm that he had managed to get.

Things gradually began to clarify in Amelia's mind. She recalled that Mama had not been entirely whole-hearted about the motor-car. She had been half-pleased the day Papa had bought it, but worried at the same time. She must have known that things were sliding downhill in Papa's business already and that buying a car wasn't a good idea. And it was the same with the gold watch that Amelia had so carelessly lost. Mama had been quite taken aback when Papa had given it to Amelia. Amelia wished she still had that watch. If the bailiffs hadn't seized it maybe she could have sold it to make a bit of extra money. But it was too late to think of that now.

Everyone in the family was very shaken by the change in their fortunes, but Papa was easily the most affected. His fair hair had lost its sheen, his brown face was now pale and drawn, his eyes looked dank and listless, and he never sang or whistled or called Amelia his princess any more. And he'd started to drink beer. He never used to before, and Amelia thought it odd that now they had less money he had found a new thing to spend it on.

And a very unpleasant thing it was too, she thought, with a nasty smell that got even nastier with the passage of time, for Papa often smelt quite disgusting in the morning after he had been drinking, and the smell of stale, spilt beer in the kitchen was suffocating. After he'd left for work, Amelia would go sniffing around till she'd found the spillage and then mop it up with water and carbolic soap. She had always hated the smell of carbolic, but now she had begun almost to like it. At least it was a clean smell, and it did a good job of abolishing the sickly-sweet, stale yeasty smell of the beer. It wasn't a case of crying over spilt milk, Amelia thought bitterly. It was crying over spilt beer that Papa had begun to make a habit of.

To make matters worse, Edmund's wretched cough just wouldn't improve. He hacked and wheezed in the night, and Amelia could hear Mama getting up to go to him. Amelia would lie in the dark and listen to the muffled choking sounds, and then the creak of a door and the rustle of Mama's dressing gown on the landing followed by the soft crooning sound of her voice as she soothed the little boy. Although Amelia felt sorry for her small brother, she wished sometimes that Mama would come with soothing sounds to her in the night.

But the very worst part about having fallen on hard times,

as Amelia liked to put it poetically to herself, was not having any servants any more. Amelia had always considered they'd had far too few, with just Cook and a maid and an outdoor man, and she couldn't imagine how they were going to manage with none at all. Cook had had no difficulty in finding a new situation. Good plain cooks with reliable references were hard to get, and there were always families on the look-out for a gem such as Cook. Mick Moriarty had taken the opportunity to go back to County Clare, where he came from, to live with his sister.

That left Mary Ann. Amelia had hoped and hoped until the very last minute that they would be able to keep Mary Ann on, even though she knew that they couldn't afford her wages, and in any case there was nowhere for a servant to sleep in the horrid new house.

'What about the attic?' Amelia suggested desperately. 'Couldn't Mary Ann sleep there?'

'Don't be absurd, Amelia,' said Papa, rather unkindly, Amelia thought. 'The attic hasn't even got a floor, not to mind a window.'

'Well then, she can share my bedroom,' she offered.

'No, Amelia,' said Mama. 'You'll have to share with Grandmama. There are only three bedrooms, and there are five in the family. The arithmetic just doesn't work out. Edmund shall have the very small room at the back.'

So Mary Ann had had to go. Mama helped her to find a situation as a tweeny, which was the very worst sort of servant to be, in a large household in Glasnevin, on the other side of the city. Amelia and she wished each other a tearful goodbye on the last day at Kenilworth Square. At least Amelia was tearful, but Mary Ann just sniffed a bit and poked Amelia in the ribs with her elbow.

'Don't worry,' she said. 'We'll still be friends. I'll train a carrier pigeon to take messages to you. Or we could learn

Morse code and send smoke signals.'

Amelia said: 'I don't think you can do that. Morse code and smoke signals are completely different things.'

'Oh lord, Amelia, where's your sense of humour? I'm warning you, if you take everything people say seriously like that you are in danger of growing up poker-faced!'

That was the last thing Mary Ann said to Amelia. But although the words were cross, she said them in a friendly tone, and Amelia knew it was her way of being kind. But with all the joking about carrier pigeons and smoke signals they didn't think of the most obvious thing – the post. Mary Ann didn't leave her new address with Amelia – to tell the truth she didn't really know the exact address in any case – and Amelia never thought of giving Mary Ann hers.

And so now the family had to struggle on as best they could without any help in the house, having lost their servants, as well as their fine house and their precious things. Most of the work fell on Mama's shoulders. She got up early in the mornings to riddle out the range. She took the hot, fuming ashes out to the yard to cool, in a metal bucket, and she brought in coke to stoke up the range again. She would pile the little round scrunchy black balls of coke into the circular fuel feed, and put the lid back on, and then she'd poke the bellows into the grid at the bottom and work the bellows good and hard to get the fire going for the breakfast. There was no point in putting a kettle or a pan onto the range until the coke was glowing bright orange.

While the range was warming up, Mama would go to the parlour and clean out that grate too, so that there'd be a little fire there for Grandmama later – Grandmama didn't move about much, and she got cold sitting still if there wasn't a fire, even in the summertime. So it was out to the yard again with the ash-bucket, and in again with the fuel. They burnt turf in the parlour fire, which smelt warm and sharp and left a soft, fine ash that created a lot of dust.

Then she'd make the breakfast. If there was milk to pour over it, she'd cook a pot of porridge. If they were short of money, and milk, she'd cut some slices of yesterday's bread and fry them in lard on a smoky hot pan. There'd be tea with the porridge or fried bread, usually with milk, sometimes black. Coffee was a thing of the past, a fragrance Amelia missed in the house at breakfast time. Tea was much cheaper, even though they had to buy it now, along with their other groceries. Papa missed the coffee too. Every morning he'd look into his breakfast cup of tea and sigh, and every time he did that, Mama winced, knowing that he was wishing it was coffee. But what could she do? It wasn't her fault they couldn't afford coffee. Nobody said anything about it, just sighed and winced.

After clearing away the breakfast there'd be more chores. On Mondays, Mama put the big tin hip-bath on the range and half-filled it with water, using buckets. She put it on before she started her breakfast, and it would take ages to boil up. Then she'd get Amelia to help her to lift it down onto a makeshift stand she made with two kitchen chairs, a hot and dangerous job. Then she'd add some bucketfuls of cold water, until the water was hand-hot – which meant unbearably hot, but not hot enough actually to bring your skin out in blisters – get the washboard out from under the sink and set to washing the family laundry. That was a long, arduous job, soaping and scrubbing and soaping and rubbing.

She rinsed everything in cold running water under the tap in the big white china sink and then took the dripping heaps of clothes out to the yard, where she fed them through the rollers of the wringer. It was hard work, turning the big cranking handle, and keeping your feet out of the way so they didn't get wet when the water came gushing out as the cloth went squeezing through. After that she had to hang them all out on the washing line and prop it up so the clothes hung high in the air where they could get a good flap.

Though he was six now and really old enough to be at school, Mama kept Edmund at home, because she thought him too delicate for the long walk there and back. That meant he was under Mama's feet all day. She tried to encourage him to stay indoors with Grandmama, but it wasn't much fun for a small boy playing quietly under the supervision of an old lady. He preferred to run under the washing line on windy days, trying to avoid the sheets that were heavy and cold with water. He laughed out loud if he got slapped by a great sopping sail of cloth, but Mama cried out crossly to him, worried on the one hand that his clothes would get damp, and on the other that contact with her son's grubby little body would streak and smudge the clean white expanses of linen and all her hard work be set at nought.

Then Mama, yelling warnings to Edmund to stand back, would pour all the filthy grey water down the drain, rinse out the bath, and begin all over again, this time boiling up Papa's shirts and the smalls. The kitchen would reek of soap and steam all day, and there'd be a slithery, soapy film on all the cold surfaces – the window-panes, the tap, the sink, even the water pipes.

'It's all *slimy*!' Edmund would squawk, turning up his nose in disgust when he came into the damp kitchen.

'You shouldn't be in here, Edmund,' Mama would retort. 'And you shouldn't be out in the back yard either. You should stay in the parlour with Grandmama, where it's warm and dry. How often do I have to tell you to keep out of my way when I'm washing?'

Edmund's nose would wrinkle up again, this time in dismay at being spoken to like this by his darling mama. Then Mama would bend down to him and scoop him up for a kiss and murmur soft apologies in his ear. She didn't know whether she was more irritated by Edmund's trailing under her feet in the tiny kitchen and yard, or worried about his chest and his persistent cough.

The next day, with a bit of luck, the clothes would all be ready for ironing. That was another day's work. First, Mama put the heavy triangular iron on to the stove to heat. Then she spread a thick, scorch-marked woollen blanket, folded over two or three times to make a heat-proof pad, on the kitchen table. When the iron smelt ready, Mama picked it up and spat on it; if the spit hissed, it was hot enough. This bit always made Edmund giggle, because he knew it was naughty to spit, and Mama would smile when he showed his shocked delight, forgiving him for having been a nuisance on wash-day.

Then it was iron, iron, as fast as she could, while the iron was hot; then put it back on the stove and wait, wait till it was hot enough to start again. She always started with a freshly heated iron on one of Papa's shirts, for these were the most important things to have perfectly smooth and with creases in the right places.

And that was only Monday's and Tuesday's work. Then there was shopping and baking – Mama was a terrible baker, and they all tried very hard to persuade her to buy shop-bread, but she would persist – and dusting and sweeping and polishing and cleaning. At least she didn't have to do the mending. Grandmama did that, and a very neat job she made of it too.

In the evenings, Mama would flop into a chair with a sigh and Amelia would make her a cup of tea and rub her shoulders, which were stiff and sore from work. All in all, poor Mama was looking the worse for wear. In the old days, she spent so much time on her projects and campaigns that she hardly had time to pay any attention to what she looked like, but nowadays she looked even worse, with her hands and wrists reddened and chapped from being constantly plunged in water, her nails cut short, her fingers nicked and scarred from sharp kitchen knives and vegetable peelers, and her hair dry and brittle from exposure to steam and kitchen dankness. Amelia was torn between guilty feelings that she ought to be helping Mama more about the house and concern for her own creamy skin and dainty hands.

She did try to do her bit now and again, and one thing she'd found she was quite good at was cooking. This was a great discovery, as Mama, though a hard worker, was a dreadful cook. Amelia said that was because she had no *feeling* for food. Mama would argue that of course she hadn't. How could anyone have a feeling for food – it was just, well, food, wasn't it? This wasn't how Amelia saw it at all, and the rest of the family, whether they had a feeling for food or not, agreed that, however poor the fare might be, Amelia was certainly the better cook. Papa and Edmund would ask anxiously who'd cooked a dish before they ventured to eat it.

'Amelia did,' Mama would always say, with a wink to Amelia, even if she'd cooked it herself, hoping they'd believe her and say the food was delicious.

'Amelia never cooked stew like this!' Papa would say, to Amelia's secret delight, pushing his plate away, and Grandmama would purse her lips, because she didn't approve of untruths, and she didn't approve of people who didn't eat their dinners either.

# Fairweather Friends

After the fiasco the birthday party had turned into, all Amelia's friends were full of curiosity about what could have befallen the Pim family so that they neglected their party guests and had the maid send them all packing. Amelia concocted a complicated lie the next day, about Papa having been taken ill, and not being able to drive any more because of it. That was how she explained the loss of the car.

When they moved house very shortly afterwards, she tried to tell her friends that it was because Papa wanted to live nearer to his business. But these stories didn't hold water for very long. Many of the girls at school came from Quaker families, and although gossiping was frowned on, it was impossible for such a big piece of news as the Pim family's financial collapse to remain a secret for long. When it emerged that Amelia Pim's father now worked for Mary Webb's father, Amelia's disgrace was complete. Everyone knew what an important businessman Charles Pim had been; it was unthinkable that he should take a paid position in someone else's firm unless something had gone seriously wrong – unless, in short, there was some truth in the rumours the young ladies of the Grosvenor Academy were imbibing with their breakfast tea.

'Melia Pim's papa stole a lot of money and was only saved from gaol by Mary Webb's father vouching for him,' they said.

''Melia Pim's papa has taken to the drink, because he can't pay his debts and his creditors are out to get him,' they hissed.

'Miss Prim-Pim, with her silk dress and her gold watch – who says that gold watch got lost? Probably pawned it to pay for the party food,' they sniggered.

'Those Pims with their motor-car and their airs and graces! They live in a hovel off the South Circular Road and have gruel and skim milk for every meal.'

'The Pim shouldn't be here at all. The Monthly Meeting pays her school fees. That's our money, you realise. Good money after bad, I call that.'

'Pim the Poorie!'

Bewildered, Amelia turned to Lucinda for comfort – funny, pretty, lively Lucinda, who would be sure to take Amelia's side and make little of her tormentors.

But Lucinda didn't see things in quite this way. Lucinda was a fun-loving creature, with a sunny nature and quick to laugh, but she reserved her quicksilver dimples and her sideways smile for those she considered worthy of them. Amelia had never noticed before how carefully Lucinda chose her place every day in class. Most people had a favourite desk, near the stove or the hot pipes in winter, near the window in summer, which they made a dive for when the bell rang. But Lucinda slipped in and out of places like a goldfish – a shimmer and a slither and she had gone, a gleam and a glide and she was somewhere else, bestowing her favours where she saw fit, turning her open gaze on whoever seemed most interesting, most well placed, most useful, perhaps.

This didn't all dawn on Amelia in a single day, of course.

She made several attempts to corner Lucinda for a chat, so she could pour her heart out to her, but every time she approached her old friend, Lucinda managed, oh so charmingly, to slip away – a music lesson here, an important engagement there, an errand to run for a teacher somewhere else. At last, Amelia got the message. Lucinda didn't want to know her any more. She, Amelia Pim, was no longer worth knowing. She had lost not only a home, wealth and security, but she had lost position in the little society of the Grosvenor Academy.

At first Amelia felt very miserable about this. She cried a lot at night, very quietly, after Grandmama had gone to sleep. One night, as Amelia was sobbing quietly into her pillow, she heard a low voice in the dark. 'I think you've cried enough now, Amelia,' Grandmama said calmly.

Amelia sat up like a shot in bed and tried to peer through the gloom to Grandmama's bed. Had she imagined it? Or had Grandmama really spoken?

At last she raised a squeaky enquiry: 'Grandmama? Are you awake?'

'Well, of course I'm awake. I don't talk in my sleep, Amelia. That's a bad habit and I don't approve of it.'

'Oh, Grandmama!' said Amelia with a soft giggle. 'Talking in their sleep isn't something a person can help!'

'Is that so?' said Grandmama.

Amelia could almost hear her smile in the darkness and realised that Grandmama had only said that to make Amelia laugh. At that moment, Amelia realised she hadn't laughed for quite a long time. This thought made her suddenly sadder than ever, and she had to make a big effort to swallow another sob.

Grandmama heard the strangled sound though, and knew that Amelia was struggling not to cry. 'That's a good girl,' she said encouragingly. 'Don't let 'em make you miserable.'

'But Grandmama,' said Amelia, mystified, 'how did you know people were making me miserable? I could have been crying about anything at all.'

'Oh no, Amelia,' came the wise old voice. 'You are a sensible girl, and sensible girls only cry about things that are worth crying about. And it's not worth crying about losing a fine house or a car or a lot of money. Those things are good, but they are not important. What's worth crying about is when you lose a friend. So I conclude that you must have lost a friend, Amelia. Or maybe more than one friend.'

'Yes, Grandmama,' whispered Amelia, feeling very strange to be sitting up in her nightgown talking to someone she couldn't see. She didn't agree that it wasn't worth crying over losing their lovely home in Kenilworth Square and the shining motor car and pots of money, but she knew Grandmama's views too well to argue.

'And was it a good, kind friend you lost, Amelia?'

Amelia thought for a moment. 'No, Grandmama,' she said slowly.

'So maybe it's not as great a loss as you imagine?'

'Maybe not, Grandmama,' said Amelia, beginning to grin a little, as she could see that Grandmama was going to *reason* her out of her misery. What a very peculiar way to comfort a person! But it was working. Already Amelia was beginning to feel lighter and brighter and altogether less despairing.

'Well, then,' said Grandmama, in a satisfied sort of tone, sounding for all the world like a barrister addressing a jury.

Amelia waited for her to say some more, but she didn't utter another sound. That was just like Grandmama. She wasn't one to chatter inconsequentially, but she knew to speak when she had something worth saying and to remain silent when she hadn't. It must have come of all those years of Quakerly silence at Meeting, Amelia thought. It was the first time she had ever seen the point of sitting still and silent.

Yes, of course, it made sense all of a sudden. If you only spoke when there really was something to say, people would naturally take you more seriously when you did speak. Am I turning into a proper Quaker at last? Amelia wondered, turning her pillow over to the dry side and beating it into shape for sleeping on.

After that, Amelia made a decision not to mind the jibes and jeers of her schoolmates. It was hard, at times, but she soon found that the best way to cope with teasing was to ignore it. Ignoring it meant not only not answering, but appearing not even to hear the insults and rude remarks they made to her or about her. When she met a girl in the corridor or sat beside one in class, she threw her a sweet, wide smile, as if they were old friends, and hurried on or buried herself in her work as if, in spite of being glad to see whoever it was, she had more important business to attend to and couldn't stop for a chat. And sure enough, after a while, they started to leave her alone.

'Grandmama?' Amelia ventured one afternoon, bringing the old lady a cup of tea in the parlour, where she sat sewing most of the day.

'Yes, Amelia,' said Grandmama, not looking up from her work, but moving some spools of thread aside to make roon for the teacup with one hand.

'Grandmama,' said Amelia again. But then she didn't quite know what she wanted to say next.

Grandmama went on sewing for a few moments, waiting for Amelia to say whatever it was she needed to say. Amelia stood there, twisting the handkerchief Mary Ann had embroidered for her birthday. After a bit, Grandmama said: 'Are you still missing your friend, Amelia?'

For a moment, Amelia thought Grandmama meant Mary Ann. But then, Grandmama wasn't looking at what Amelia was twisting in her hands, so she couldn't realise that Amelia was thinking of the servant girl. No, Grandmama must mean Lucinda, who, as Grandmama had pointed out before, was no great loss, not being a good, kind friend.

'Well,' she said, 'it's not so much that I miss *her* exactly. It's more that I just miss having a friend, Grandmama.'

'It's hard not to have a friend among your peers, Amelia.'

This sounded very grave, so Amelia responded gravely: 'Yes, Grandmama.'

'And are they still teasing you, Amelia?'

How did Grandmama know they'd been teasing her, Amelia wondered. She hadn't mentioned that part of it.

'Oh no, Grandmama, they've given up,' she said.

'Good. That means you must have been sticking it out bravely and seeming not to mind. Because that's the only way to deal with bullying and meanness. If you seem not to care, they soon lose interest in teasing you. There is no satisfaction to be gained from teasing someone who appears not to mind. That's a good strategy, Amelia.'

Amelia smiled a pleased smile to herself. That was a long speech, for Grandmama. It didn't make it easier to hear that she was doing the right thing, but it helped to make her feel a little better.

In fact, not only had the girls stopped teasing her; some of them had actually begun to admire her. They didn't go so far as to try to befriend her again – Lucinda wouldn't tolerate that – but they sometimes returned her smiles of greeting, or at least had the grace to look sheepish.

Dorothea Jacob looked the most sheepish of all when she met Amelia in school. In fact, she looked not so much like a sheep as like a rabbit that's had a scare, and she made an effort to scamper away every time she saw Amelia. Amelia sometimes wondered what it was about herself that seemed to unsettle Dorothea so, but she didn't give it too much thought.

What was exercising her mind now was how to make contact with Mary Ann. This was the subject she had wanted to raise with Grandmama, but she felt shy of asking. While the teasing and nastiness were going on at school, and as she smarted with the hurt of Lucinda's rejection, Amelia's thoughts turned more and more to Mary Ann. Mary Ann could always make her laugh when she was feeling low. She thought about the day she had comforted Mary Ann when her mother had been ill; she thought about the glorious day they had polished the orangery together; and she thought with special fondness and gratitude of the way Mary Ann had taken over when Amelia had gone to pieces at the birthday party; and she was filled with longing to see her friend.

But how was she going to arrange it? She'd been hoping and hoping for a letter. Every morning she got up early – she wasn't sleeping well anyway in the new house, not being used to living practically on the street – and crept downstairs before the others were up, every morning expecting to find a letter from Mary Ann. But every morning there was no letter. Every morning that there was no letter increased the chances that there'd be one on the next morning, Amelia told herself. But as the weeks went by, with still no sound from her friend, Amelia had to face it: either Mary Ann didn't know where Amelia lived now, or she just didn't want to write. She couldn't bear to think that Mary Ann didn't want to keep in touch. She had promised, after all. It must be that she didn't know the address. The only thing for it was for Amelia to find out Mary Ann's address and to write to her or visit her instead.

She knew Mary Ann worked for a family called Shackleton, acquaintances of her parents, but she didn't know exactly where they lived. The obvious thing would be to ask Mama if she could find out and arrange for Amelia to visit

Mary Ann or for Mary Ann to visit them. But she was a little afraid of asking Mama. Mama mightn't think it was such a good idea. Of course Mama had what were known as very 'advanced' views, which meant that she treated her servants like human beings and didn't hold with old-fashioned notions of whom it was appropriate to mix with, but even so, she might think it would be unsettling for Mary Ann in her new situation to be approached by Amelia. And then, if Amelia did ask Mama, and Mama forbade her to contact Mary Ann, she'd be stumped. No, she wouldn't say a word to Mama, just in case. She wouldn't want to risk being told that she mustn't. She would just have to think up some other way of tracking Mary Ann down.

# Mama's Speech

One afternoon, there was no sign of Mama when Amelia came home from school. This was not unusual. If she got time, Mama often slipped out in the afternoon and went to a meeting or a rally in town. She was usually home by five or so. When Mama hadn't turned up by half past five, Amelia bustled into the kitchen and looked for an apron to cover her school smock with. She found one Mama had stitched out of old flourbags, tied it around her body and set to getting the family's evening meal ready.

Separate supper for the grown-ups had been done away with long ago, and no-one had proper tea any more. Everyone helped themselves to a cup from the teapot on the little low range when they came in, and cut themselves a slice of bread, if there was any, and whoever happened to be around took a cup to Grandmama, who sat in the tiny front parlour most of the day. And then they all had a hot meal at about seven. Sometimes there was bacon or kippers or stew with a lot of onions and a little meat. Occasionally there was a nice lentil or split-pea soup, if there had been bacon earlier in the week and Mama had remembered to save the bone for stock. Sometimes there was only potatoes and cabbage. One awful Friday, when Papa had dropped into the pub and forgotten to come home, there had been only porridge.

Amelia first put on the kettle to boil and then she took a coarse basket from under the sink and went out to the shed, where a sack of potatoes leant darkly against a corner. She fished out the heavy, earthy vegetables one by one, counting under her breath as she filled her basket. They were cold and crumbly to the touch and mouldy to the nose. Amelia didn't like the smell of earth and sacking, but she knew the potatoes underneath would be clean and fresh. Even though there was no meat today, Amelia was determined to make a tasty meal. She knew there was a nice half-pound of butter keeping cool in the safe in a sunless corner of the yard, and with a pinch of salt and a lump of that good yellow butter, the potatoes would be delicious, washed down with some milk. Was there enough milk, she wondered, or would she have to water it a bit to stretch it? She was becoming quite the little housekeeper.

As Amelia scrubbed away, trying not to notice how black her fingernails were getting from the spuds, Mama whirled in, hot and breathless, her cheeks on fire and her hair coming down on one side as usual. She threw herself into a kitchen chair and gasped for breath. She'd clearly been running. She must have realised she was late.

'You are a darling child, Amelia,' she said when she got her breath back.

Yes, thought Amelia proudly, I am rather, aren't I? Well, she was a good cook, and what was more she was a willing cook, and she did get on with what had to be done without even being asked.

'Did you remember to fill the kettle first, though?' Mama went on.

'Yes, Mama,' said Amelia.

Mama was terribly keen to show off how good she was in the kitchen. Only last week she had worked out that it saved time if you put on the water for the potatoes first, before you scrubbed them. That way the water boiled as you scrubbed, and you didn't have to sit around waiting for it. She had pointed this out to Amelia as if it were a revolutionary idea. Amelia very kindly didn't say that this was perfectly obvious to any but the most incompetent person.

Mama eased off her boots and reached under the chair to where she kept an old pair of indoor shoes, shabby and shapeless and quite disgraceful to look at, but very comfortable.

'Have you been to a meeting, Mama?' asked Amelia, tilting the great iron kettle to fill a saucepan for the potatoes.

'How did you guess?' Mama looked genuinely surprised.

'Oh, it's the particular way your hair hangs down when you get excited. Was it exciting?'

'Well,' said Mama, drawing on her indoor shoes, 'it was certainly invigorating. I'm afraid I made a speech, dear.'

'On the rights of women, I suppose,' said Amelia, with a resigned air. She tolerated Mama's feminist views, but she found it all very dreary.

'No,' said Mama, and paused. 'No. This speech was on the rights of all human beings. It was on the right to stay alive, as a matter of fact. You know the Countess Constance Markievicz?'

'Oh yes. The one with the soup-kitchen and the army of little boys. The one that dressmaker disapproved of, the day I went to have my dress fitted. Do you remember my green silk?' Amelia's voice took on a dreamy tone. She almost over-filled the potato pot.

'Well, she and a group of other women have got together to form a women's society. Cumann na mBan they call it. That means the company of women. Isn't that a fine-sounding name?'

Amelia didn't think so. She thought it sounded deadly dull,

a lot of earnest women in serge skirts and horn-rimmed spectacles smelling not quite fresh and dainty, endlessly *talking*, so she didn't say anything.

'I wanted to see Constance again. I hadn't spoken to her since we worked together at Liberty Hall during the lock-out, feeding the men who were out of work and their families. And I thought this Cumann na mBan business might be interesting. I mean, I knew it was for Nationalist women, but I thought that as women, they might bring a fresh way of thinking to the whole Nationalist issue.'

'What do you mean, a fresh way of thinking?' Mama said the oddest things sometimes, Amelia thought.

But Mama wasn't listening. She was bursting to tell her daughter about the meeting.

'But oh, Amelia!' she exclaimed. 'They want to make soldiers of themselves! To fight the British.'

This was a strange idea. Women soldiers. Amelia tried to imagine battalions of women, marching in battle dress, carrying guns, but she couldn't.

'That is not what women should be doing.' Mama was thumping the table and speaking in a loud, rousing voice, as if she were addressing a meeting, not her own daughter in her own kitchen. 'Women should be trying to persuade their men-folk not to go to war, not encouraging them in their daft and bloody ideals.'

'Mary Ann says that Ireland unfree will never be at peace,' Amelia said, suddenly making a link between what Mama was saying and her old friend. Mary Ann was always going on about the Nationalist cause and making veiled remarks about guns and fighting.

Mama didn't seem to notice how Amelia had slipped Mary Ann's name into the conversation.

'I am as anxious to see Ireland free as the next person,' she went on, still addressing an imaginary audience. 'But this isn't the time to start a revolution. And anyway, I shall never believe that you achieve peace through violence.'

At this point, Mama smacked her boot, which she was still holding in one hand, smartly down on the table top. Her eyes were shining and her lock of escaped hair had slapped itself across her face and plastered itself over her mouth, so that she looked as if she had been gagged. 'Eugh!' she exclaimed, poking hair out her mouth.

Amelia was at a bit of a loss. She wasn't entirely clear what Mama was on about. So she asked what seemed to her the obvious question: 'Did you speak to the Countess?'

'No. She gave me a fiery look when I said my piece and she swept past me when she left.'

'But you used to be friends, Mama.' Amelia felt strongly about friendship just now, and she couldn't keep a sad note out of her voice.

'No. We were never that, Amelia. I admired her. I still do. Her work in the women's suffrage movement was wonderful in the old days. She has high ideals and she really cares. But she has some wild and dangerous ideas too, and I can't go along with her when it comes to guns and armies. We were comrades once, not friends. And my understanding of comradeship doesn't stretch to the military meaning of the word.'

'Mama, do you think someone like Mary Ann might join an organisation like that comin' thing you were talking about?'

'Mary Ann? I doubt it.' Mama didn't sound very interested. She suddenly looked very tired and worried, and she sat down heavily on a kitchen chair and asked: 'Is there any tea in that pot, or is it stewed to gravy?'

Amelia had been half-hoping Mama might have met Mary Ann at the meeting, if it was one for women interested in the Nationalist cause. She knew Mary Ann held Nationalist views, but it had only been an off-chance that Mama might have spotted her there.

How was she ever going to trace Mary Ann without asking Mama directly? And she didn't think she could do that. Look how Mama had brushed off her tentative enquiry. No. Mama didn't want to encourage Amelia to seek out Mary Ann. That much was clear.

# The Telephone Call

Amelia had had a brilliant idea. The Shackletons were a rich family, she knew, with a big business in town. And they had a car and a reputation for being modern. With a little bit of luck, they would have a telephone. Not many people had telephones in their private houses. But an important businessman might have one.

Now, if they had a telephone, all Amelia had to do was find out the telephone number and ring them up and ask to speak to Mary Ann. What could be simpler? She gave herself a little hug when she thought of it.

But how did you find out somebody's telephone number? It wouldn't be in Thom's Directory in the library. That was only for street addresses, as far as she knew. Was there some sort of an equivalent directory for telephone numbers, Amelia wondered? She wished they'd had a telephone in Kenilworth Square when they'd been rich, so that she would be *au fait* with how they worked. But Grandmama said telephones were instruments of the devil, invented to encourage idle chatter, and that if anyone needed to get a message to them in a hurry, they could send a telegram, as civilised people did. Besides, telegrams kept telegraph boys in employment, Grandmama reasoned. You mark her words, but if ever these telephone machines caught on good and proper there'd be no more work for those lads.

That was all very well, but the upshot of it was that Amelia hadn't the least idea how to use a telephone, or even how to find out a telephone number. Never mind, she would go to the General Post Office and someone there would be sure to be able to help her.

So one afternoon after school, instead of going home directly, she caught a tram at Portobello Bridge and made a little expedition into town. The tram followed the same route it had on that day she had gone to town with Mama for the silk for her party dress, the day Mama had given her her lucky sixpence. She had put the little silver coin away carefully that evening, thinking that since it was a special sixpence she had come by completely unexpectedly, she mustn't spend it on peggy's legs or toffee or aniseed balls or any of the usual things she spent her pennies on, but she must keep it for some day in the future, when she might have a particular use for it. As soon as Amelia thought of the plan of telephoning Mary Ann, she realised the day had come to spend her lucky sixpence. She wouldn't have had the tram-fare otherwise, and she hadn't time to walk all the way.

Amelia stepped down from the tram at the Pillar and tripped across the road to the GPO. It was a great imposing building, with pillars that went up and up, and revolving doors like glass capsules that trapped you inside, forced you around and spat you out the other side. Inside, it was all marble and mahogany and brass, and a hollow, echoing sound of people talking and cash boxes snapping shut. She joined a short queue at a grille that was manned by a youngish, friendly fellow, who looked as if he wouldn't mind explaining about telephoning to a nervous girl. While she waited, Amelia admired the gleaming brass rods that separated the clerks from the public. Funny – a few weeks ago she would probably not even have seen the brass; but now she knew just how much Brasso and elbow grease it took to keep brass bright and yellow like that, and suddenly she appreciated it.

The clerk looked up the telephone number for her. 'Shackleton, Charles; Shackleton, Jonathan; Shackleton, William,' he rattled off.

'Oh dear,' said Amelia. 'I don't know which one it is.'

'You mean you don't know who it is you want to ring up?' asked the clerk in surprise.

'Not really,' admitted Amelia.

This seemed to amuse the clerk.

'Perhaps it's the father's name you don't know,' he said waggishly. 'Maybe it's young Master Shackleton you're interested in, is that right?'

'Oh, is there a young Master Shackleton?' said Amelia.

'My, but you're a cool one,' said the clerk. 'Look, give us a clue.'

Amelia was standing first on one foot and then on the other, as she did when she was agitated. She thought the clerk was trying to play some sort of little game with her, but she didn't know the rules. She wished she did know, so she could make the right move next and get the information she needed.

'What sort of a clue?'

'Well, is it the Kingstown Shackletons you want, or the Rathfarnham Shackletons, or the Glasnevin Shackletons?'

'Glasnevin! That's it. Oh, thank you!' Amelia beamed at the clerk.

He thought she was a funny sort of an elf to be out on her own looking for a telephone number, but he wrote it down for her, in pencil on a torn-off piece of newspaper.

'What do I do now?' she asked.

'You ring them up,' he said slowly.

'Yes, but how?'

She really was a rum one, he thought. 'Look, you take the number to that lady over there. She'll tell you what to do. Next!' The last word was directed loudly and firmly over Amelia's shoulder to the person behind her, who had been shuffling and sighing for some time.

Amelia stumbled across the great hall to the lady the clerk had pointed out.

'I'd like to telephone this number, please,' she said, handing over the scrap of paper.

'Booth 5!' said the lady telephonist loudly, to no-one in particular.

Amelia looked around her. There was nobody there but herself.

'Booth 5?' she said.

'Yes.'

Amelia had no idea what she meant. She looked enquiringly at the telephonist, who pointed to a row of upright wooden coffins with windows, against a wall.

'One of those?' Amelia asked, her mouth dry.

'Booth 5. You know, 1, 2, 3, 4, 5.' The telephonist counted out the numbers on her fingers, as if Amelia were a foreigner or an idiot.

'Yes, yes,' she said, and drifted off to booth 5.

She creaked the door open and went in. It was dark and stuffy inside and she couldn't see a thing. Just then the door clicked shut behind her and an electric light came on, right above her head. Amelia gave a little scream. She had never seen an electric light bulb up close before – they'd had gas in the main rooms in Kenilworth Square, and they only had oil-lamps in Lombard Street – and she had no idea that an electric light switch could be wired up to a door, so it seemed to her as if the light had come on by supernatural means.

Luckily nobody heard her scream. It was only a little scream, and the door was stout, so she was insulated from the world outside. She peered out through the glass panels and looked at the people going about their business, quite unaware that Amelia Pim was having a trying afternoon. This must be what it was like to be a goldfish, able to see the outside world, but able to hear it only in a muffled way. Just then there was a shrill ringing sound. Amelia almost jumped out of her skin. The high-pitched ring came again. She reached out for the telephone with a trembling hand. She thought *she* was going to ring *them*, so how was it that *they* were ringing *her*? Just as she was about to pick up the ear-piece the telephone gave another piercing squeal, as if it was impatient with her. She snatched the ear-piece from the hook and tried to reach the mouthpiece, but it was too high for her. She had to stand on tiptoe and shout into it.

'Yes?'

'Your call is through now, caller. Thank you.'

'Oh, thank you,' said Amelia loudly into the mouthpiece.

'I beg your pardon?' came a man's voice. 'This is the Shackleton residence. May I help you?'

'Oh!' said Amelia. 'Yes.'

'Well?'

'Could I speak to Mary Ann, please.'

'I'm afraid you must have a wrong connection. I'm so sorry. This is the Shackleton residence.'

'Yes, I know,' said Amelia. 'Does Mary Ann Maloney not work there?'

'Maloney? The under-housemaid! Good heavens, we don't take telephone calls for the servants!'

'Please, don't hang up.' Amelia thought fast. 'I'm sorry to bother you, but you see I'm afraid it's an emergency.'

'Emergency? What sort of emergency can there possibly be that requires the tweeny to come to the telephone?'

'It's her mother,' said Amelia quickly. 'She's very ill. She may not last the night. Please let me talk to her.'

'Very well. You may have three minutes.'

It must be the butler, Amelia thought. Nobody else would be so pompous. A real gentleman would never refer to his own house as his 'residence'.

'Hello?' Mary Ann's voice sounded very tiny and wobbly.

'It's all right, Mary Ann. There's nothing wrong with your mother. It's me, Amelia.'

'Amelia!' Mary Ann's voice still sounded wobbly.

'Is that horrid butler listening?'

'Yes,' said Mary Ann.

'Botheration! Now listen, I'll do the talking in that case. You just say Yes and No. All right?'

'Yes.'

'I told him your mother was ill. Did he tell you that?'

'Yes.'

'Sorry. She's not. I just had to make that up to get him to let you come to the telephone. Oh, Mary Ann! I need to see you. I miss you. How are you?'

'Yes,' said Mary Ann.

Amelia started to giggle. 'Have you got time off on Sunday?'

'No.'

'Not even on Sundays!'

'Yes,' said Mary Ann.

This was getting very confusing.

Amelia had a brainwave. 'You mean you have time off on some Sundays?'

'Yes.'

'But not this Sunday coming?'

'No.'

'The one after that then?'

'Yes.'

'In the afternoon?' This was hard work!

'Yes.'

'Can you meet me somewhere?'

'Yes.'

Bother and double-bother! How was Amelia ever going to make a complicated arrangement like this with someone who could only answer Yes or No?

'He's gone!' Mary Ann's voice came suddenly rapidly and more loudly. 'Sunday week, two o'clock, outside the Metropole hotel. Goodbye.'

'Mary Ann, where are ... oh!' There was only a buzzing sound from the instrument. Mary Ann had gone.

Amelia stood there for a moment, overcome by the excitement of it all. Then she hung the telephone receiver up on its little hook again, and pushed her way out of the telephone booth.

Well, that hadn't been so bad. Now all she needed to do was to make sure she was at the hotel on Sunday week. She was sure she could manage that. She'd managed to make a telephone call all by herself, hadn't she? She felt quite satisfied with herself as she crossed the marble floor again towards the revolving door.

'Miss! Hey you! Miss!'

Amelia stopped in her tracks. Could they mean her? What had she done? She looked back to see the telephonist waving angrily at her.

'You there! You didn't pay for your telephone call!'

Amelia was mortified. People would think she was trying to cheat. She ran back to the counter, wishing the woman would stop shouting. Everyone was looking at her. That's Amelia Pim, they were thinking. Trying to pull a fast one. I wouldn't trust those Pims. They don't pay their debts.

She was almost in tears when she reached the telephonist. 'I'm so sorry! I'm most terribly sorry! I didn't know.'

'I suppose you thought telephone calls were free, gratis and for nothing? Courtesy of His Majesty's Government?'

'No. I just didn't think.'

'Didn't think is no excuse. Think the next time, young missy. That'll be a penny ha'penny, please.'

Amelia poked the coins out of her purse and fled from the GPO, swirling through the revolving doors and out with a clunk onto the pavement. She ran all the way to College Green, fleeing from the feeling of being watched and pointed at. At last she stopped to catch her breath. The streets were busy: men were shouting at horses and women were calling to children, hurrying them along, and trams were clanging by at a great rate. It was the end of the working day, and everyone was scurrying home to their tea. Nobody had time to stop and wonder about Amelia Pim. She slowed down to a walk. She might as well walk the rest of the way, as she had come so far, and save the rest of her money for another day.

What an adventure it had all been! But it had been worth it. She'd got to talk to Mary Ann. And now she had a meeting with her friend to look forward to.

# Shocking News

Amelia was getting more enterprising as she became more experienced in the kitchen, and one particular evening she was experimenting with potato cakes, and making excellent progress too. She heard Mama's key in the door and she looked up, ready to smile at her and tell her all about the potato-cake recipe.

But it was Papa's frame that filled the kitchen doorway, and Papa's eyes she met when she looked up.

'Hello, Papa.' Amelia smiled up at him. 'You're early.'

'Yes,' he said, not moving from the doorway.

'Well, do come in and sit down, Papa,' said Amelia pleasantly. 'There's tea in the pot if you'd like to help yourself.'

Still, Papa didn't move from the doorway.

'Please, Papa, there's a draught with the door open like that. Maybe you're too tired to get your own tea. If you just sit at the table, I'll pour you a cup in half a tick, as soon as I get this flour off my hands. It makes a dreadful mess, flour does, Papa. And the problem is that when you try to wash it off it all turns into paste on your hands, and it takes ages to get rid of it.' Amelia was prattling away and scrubbing at her hands as she spoke. She had her back to Papa.

'Now, then,' she said, turning around with the kitchen

towel in her hands and drying between her fingers. 'Why, Papa! Why on earth don't you come in and sit down? I told you, you're making a draught, standing in the open doorway like that.'

Something was wrong. It wasn't quite like the afternoon of the bankruptcy, but there was something familiar about the way Papa's eyes looked. He was standing stock still.

Amelia went to him, caught him by the elbow and drew him into the kitchen, shutting the door as soon as she got an opportunity. She guided Papa to the table and pulled out a chair for him.

'Now, tell me what the matter is, Papa,' she said in a soft voice, as if she were speaking to Edmund when he was feeling unwell.

Papa said nothing. He shook his head.

'Is someone ill? Has someone had an accident?'

He shook his head again.

'Well, that's good,' said Amelia. 'That's the worst it could be, and it's not that. Isn't that so, Papa? Now, have you a problem at work? You haven't been dismissed, Papa?' Her voice was lower than ever now. Amelia was convinced it was something like that. Perhaps Papa had been up to his old tricks, spending money he really hadn't got. Surely, surely he wouldn't actually steal money?

'No,' said Papa at last.

'And it's nothing at all to do with work?'

'No,' he said again.

'Or money, Papa? It hasn't anything to do with money or debts or a bill you can't pay, Papa?'

He shook his head again.

Amelia thought for a bit. Then she stood up and poured her father's tea. A cup of tea might do him good, and anyway she found it comforting to do something normal like pouring tea. But every time she made a pot of tea now or even poured a cup, Amelia would blush inwardly, remembering the day Mama had announced so blithely to the shopboy in Findlater's that they were Pims the tea merchants, when obviously the lad had been warned that the Pims weren't to be extended credit any longer; there must have been a big unsettled account at that shop.

She put the tea in front of Papa, and stirred two spoons of sugar into it for him.

'Drink it, Papa,' she said.

He took the teacup in both hands and drank gratefully. Then he pushed it away from him and laid both arms on the table and sank his head onto them. He said nothing for a while, and Amelia sat and waited. Without sitting up, he started to pat the table blindly with one hand, as if looking for something. Amelia understood. She put her hand out, palm down, on the table, in reach of his patting hand. When he found it, he closed his big brown hand over her little one, and gave it a very gentle squeeze.

They sat in silence for a bit longer, then Papa sighed and lifted his head.

'Your mother has got herself arrested for a breach of the peace,' he said quietly.

Arrested! Amelia's face flushed hot and her heart beat hard. Mama! Papa was the one Amelia had worried about getting into trouble with the law. Sometimes she had been afraid that the rumours she heard at school were true, and that Papa had not only made bad business decisions but had actually done something dishonest. She hadn't wanted to believe it, but it was a niggling little thought that sometimes bothered her. But *Mama*! The last thing she had ever expected of passionate, concerned, philanthropic, peace-loving Mama was that she would get arrested. Amelia felt as if her world, already shaken by recent events, had now turned completely upside down.

She didn't say anything. She couldn't. She moved her small hand, where it still lay under Papa's, and she in her turn squeezed his hand.

'How did you hear, Papa?' she asked at last.

'From Bertie Fry. He sent a telegram to the office. You're allowed to send for your solicitor if you're arrested. So Mama sent for Bertie, and he sent me a telegram to tell me she was in Mountjoy Gaol.'

Arrested! The word, and the idea, struck Amelia again, more forcefully than before. This was worse than bankruptcy. In Mountjoy! Mama was in prison! Like a common criminal! Oh, how would they ever live it down! Everyone would get to hear about it. There might be policemen arriving at their door at any minute. The neighbours would see. What ever were they going to do?

'I'm going to go over to Mountjoy now,' said Papa, 'and see if they'll let me talk to her. She's appearing in court in the morning.'

Tomorrow morning. That meant ... that meant Mama was actually going to have to sleep in the prison. What would that be like? Would she have a proper bed with a mattress? Would she have to share with other people? Would she have a wc, or would she have to use a smelly old bucket? Would she have to drink out of a little tin cup, like a child? Oh, poor Mama!

'I'll get her things,' Amelia said at last, standing up.

'What things?' Papa looked stupidly at his daughter. He must be quite worn out, thought Amelia.

'A nightgown, Papa, clean things. A toothbrush, a hairbrush, a nailbrush, a hand-mirror.' Amelia was imagining Mama with no-one to tell her that her hair was coming down. 'Extra hairpins, some rosewater, cotton wool, face cream.'

'Face cream! Your mother has been arrested and is in prison and you want to send her face cream!'

'Oh Papa! I don't know what else to do!' Amelia wailed. Sending face cream to Mama was the best she could think of. It wasn't fair of Papa to upbraid her for that; if she were in prison, she'd like someone to send her face cream. If she could think of something more useful, why, she'd send it.

But that wasn't what Papa meant at all.

'I told her!' he went on angrily, ignoring Amelia's reply. 'I told her it would come to this. I warned her, over and over. I said the authorities wouldn't put up with it. They've done it before, you know, arrested these suffragettes with their chains and their stones and their ridiculous placards. Votes for women, indeed! If they stayed at home and looked after their families they wouldn't need votes. They'd be happy, doing the work God intended women to do. They shouldn't be out on the streets trying to disrupt the natural order.'

Amelia gaped at Papa. She had never heard him express opinions like this. The most he'd ever done before was rag Mama gently about her activities, and she would smile at him and ruffle his hair and tell him he was a boring old fossil.

Something happened inside Amelia's head, or perhaps it was inside her heart, when she heard Papa say these things. Quite suddenly, she stopped feeling ashamed to be the daughter of a person who was in prison. She was confused about Mama's feminist views, she wasn't at all sure whether she agreed with votes for women, and she certainly disapproved of people making asses of themselves on the streets; but when she heard Papa making disparaging remarks about Mama's deeply held convictions, she felt hurt and angry on Mama's behalf, and she wanted to rush to Mama's defence.

She was quite sure Mama hadn't done anything foolish or outrageous or violent. She wouldn't throw stones at policemen or shout insults at members of parliament or break windows or any of those things. She would deport herself with decorum, even if she were carrying a placard on the streets. And if Mama felt strongly enough about votes for women to be out on the streets carrying placards, well, then, it must be important. That was good enough for Amelia. All at once she understood that Mama's views must be worth fighting for. Not fighting for in the way Mary Ann's brother felt he had to fight for his Nationalist beliefs, but fighting for in Mama's gentle, pacifist, protesting way. And if Papa didn't agree, then that was a shame – but it was a shame about Papa, not a shame about Mama.

She left the kitchen without saying anything and went upstairs to her parents' room. She got together all the things she had mentioned to Papa, packing the toiletries into a spongebag and stuffing the lot into the smallest suitcase she could find. She looked around to see what else Mama might like. There was a pile of books by Mama's bed. She chose two: *A Vindication of the Rights of Women* by somebody called Mary Wollstonecraft, and Mama's well-thumbed copy of the Bible.

She came downstairs to the kitchen and looked about for some food to pack. She had heard that prisoners were expected to live on bread and water. She found an orange and a slab of chocolate Grandmama had bought as a treat for Edmund, and she cut two rounds of bread. There wasn't anything to make a sandwich with, so she just spread blackcurrant jam thickly on the bread and she wrapped it up in wax paper. She almost wished Mama were a man, because then she could send her some tobacco. At the last moment, Amelia had a thought. She tore a strip off a stout paper bag and made a little poke out of it, into which she carefully poured a handful of sugar. They'd be sure to give her tea in prison – surely the stories about bread and water couldn't be true, not in the twentieth century – but they mightn't give her sugar for it, and Mama had a sweet tooth. She packed all the foodstuffs into a little egg-basket.

'There!' she said, handing the lot over to Papa.

Papa took the small battered suitcase and the little basket of food, and he smiled sheepishly at Amelia, apparently a little ashamed of his earlier outburst.

'You're a good girl, Amelia Pim,' he said in his best Papa-ish voice. 'You're a princess,' he added.

He hadn't called her that for a long, long time. Then he leant over and kissed his daughter lightly on the forehead. Amelia forgave him at once: she knew he'd said those hurtful things only because he was worried about Mama, and worried about the family having to soldier on without her while she was away.

'Give her my best love, Papa,' said Amelia. 'And tell her I'm proud of her.'

Papa gave her a strange look, but he said nothing.

At the door Papa turned. Amelia had gone back to her potato cakes.

'Save me some supper,' he said.

'Yes, Papa.'

'Papa!' Amelia called, as he turned away again. 'What'll I tell Grandmama? Oh Papa,' and her voice became tearful as she suddenly thought of her little brother, 'what ever shall I say to Edmund?'

Papa looked back at her, a long, weary look.

'Tell Grandmama the truth, of course,' he said at last. 'But Edmund ... I don't know, Amelia. Whatever you think. I leave it up to you. Say whatever you think best.'

# Night Alarm

Papa was allowed to see Mama that evening, but only because she hadn't appeared before the magistrate yet. He came home late, carrying the little brown suitcase Amelia had given him. In it were most of the things Amelia had sent to Mama. She was only allowed a minimum of personal effects, and hairpins and hand-mirrors were apparently considered dangerous in the hands of prisoners.

But Mama had evidently been glad of the food Amelia had sent. At least, it hadn't come back with the other things. She had been allowed to keep the Bible also. Amelia was glad about that. It wasn't a book she read much herself, but she knew Mama liked to find solace there at times. Amelia wished with all her heart that it would bring Mama some comfort in that dark, clanging place where they had locked her up.

Papa attended the court hearing the following day. Mama was convicted of a breach of the peace and sentenced to sixty days in prison. Now she would have to wear prison clothes – a coarse cotton skirt and blouse, printed with arrows. Amelia wept at the thought.

Sixty days didn't sound too bad, but it was a long time for the family to be without a mother, and a long, dreary time for Mama with no-one to talk to and nothing much to do, and visits from Papa only very seldom.

Amelia got angry every time she thought of Mama being locked up for doing nothing more riotous than carrying a placard. Some of the other women she had been with at the rally outside the Vice-Regal Lodge had apparently got a little excited and had waved their placards rather fiercely, and one of them had threatened to bring hers down with a smash on a policeman's helmeted head. But, exactly as Amelia had imagined, Mama had done nothing more offensive than chant 'Votes for Women' as she walked up and down, and not even the police or the courts could say otherwise.

Amelia knew all this because there was an account of the trial in the newspaper. The report didn't say anything about how the women should have been at home making their husbands' tea, even though that might have been what the reporter thought privately. The editor even went so far as to say that it was a poor day for Ireland when protesting peaceably was considered a crime worthy of imprisonment, even if it was outside the Lord Lieutenant's gate. 'Good for you!' Amelia whispered to the editor as she read this bit, and she hoped there was some spiritual system whereby feelings of goodwill could be transmitted to the appropriate quarter.

Amelia had had a little moment of panic when she first saw the report in the paper. She thought of all the breakfast tables this very report would be read at. She imagined Lucinda and Dorothea and Mary and the others, all hearing their papas reading the newspaper account out to a hushed family, and the little smiles of satisfaction that might be hidden behind breakfast napkins. The Pims were well and truly disgraced now. The father had escaped prison by the skin of his teeth, but now the mother had gone and landed herself in Mountjoy, and that was even worse. How extremely unladylike of her!

But then Amelia shook herself hard and resolved to hold

her head up and not to allow herself to think such thoughts. The girls at school could look down on her all they liked, but she knew her mother had done nothing wrong. All she had done was express her opinions, a little publicly, perhaps, but that was no crime – or at least it jolly well oughtn't to be.

Amelia hadn't gone to school the previous day of course. She had waited with Grandmama for Papa to come home with the news from the court. Edmund was playing in the hall. He'd found an old wooden crate and he was sitting in it, swaying from side to side with a serious expression on his face and making chuff-chuff noises. When Papa had come in, he'd had to pretend to be the station master and blow an imaginary whistle, on Edmund's instructions. It was some time before he could slip away and break the news to the womenfolk, who sat patiently in the kitchen.

'Amelia had better stay home from school for a bit,' Papa said. 'Somebody has to keep house until Roberta gets home. Edmund needs looking after and there's the cooking and everything.'

'What about the girl's education?' said Grandmama in an outraged tone. Grandmama was a great believer in girls' education.

'It'll have to wait,' said Papa. 'She's needed here now.'

'Well, I can't say I approve,' said Grandmama. 'Schooling's important.'

'Home's important too,' said Papa. 'Especially for a girl.'

Amelia wasn't sure what he meant by that, and Grandmama glowered, but staying at home appealed to Amelia. She didn't set much store by education herself, though she quite enjoyed school, and she was terribly pleased to be needed at home.

Of course, she was sorry not to have the opportunity to hold her head up in front of the others, but she knew she would get that opportunity eventually, and in the meantime she would practise holding her head up at home, on the streets and in the shops. Her neck would develop enlarged muscles, she thought ruefully to herself, from all the holding up it was going to have to do.

One evening, as Amelia was putting the porridge oats to steep for the next morning's breakfast, the last of the evening chores, and longing to slip off to bed, she heard a sudden thump upstairs. The stairs went up at the back of the house, rising from the kitchen, where Amelia was working, so she could hear what went on on the landing almost as if it were in the same room.

'Edmund!' she called out. The little boy had picked at his dinner even more fitfully than usual that evening and he had dragged himself off to bed early.

There was no reply. Amelia wondered if Edmund had dropped a book. Yet it had sounded too muffled a thump for a book. Yes, a falling book sounded sharper, more defined. This was more like – well, it was more like a body collapsing. Surely Edmund was too old for falling out of bed!

Amelia yawned and put the porridge pot on the drainer by the sink. She wiped her hands quickly on her apron and skipped up the stairs to investigate.

But she didn't get as far as Edmund's room. She almost fell over him on the landing, where he lay in a heap, with his dressing-gown partly on and partly off. For a moment, Amelia stood looking down at him, wondering how he could have got there. If he'd fallen out of bed, he could hardly have rolled all this way.

But of course, Edmund couldn't possibly have fallen out of bed. He had been pulling his dressing-gown on when he fell. He must have been on his way to the lavatory, or downstairs for a drink.

Amelia bent down and lifted up the little body. He was surprisingly light, like a rather large doll. She carried him into the bedroom, laid him on the bed, and ran downstairs for the oil-lamp, as Edmund's candle was out. When she arrived back in his room, Edmund was moving about, like a fish on a riverbank, floppy and nervy. Well, at least he was alive. She leant over him and spoke his name. He opened his eyes, but he didn't seem to see her, even though she was holding the lamp. She stood the lamp carefully on the tallboy and came back to the bed. 'Edmund!' she called again. This time his eyes seemed to focus on her, but after a moment they closed again, as if the effort was too much for him. He was only half-conscious, she realised, and his breathing was very rapid. She felt for his pulse. It was racing. And he must be feverish. His cheeks were pale, but his forehead was hot to the touch, and his hair was plastered over his brow with perspiration.

Amelia wrapped the dressing-gown more closely around her brother and she tucked him under the blankets. She felt around for the crockery jar she had filled for him earlier. It was still warm, making a hard lumpiness under the bottom sheet, where she put it to protect his feet from being scalded by it.

Leaving the lamp burning in the room and the door open so she could benefit from its light, she groped her way in the shadows down the stairs to get her coat and hat. Then she went in to Grandmama, who was nodding in an armchair by the embers of the parlour fire. 'Grandmama,' she whispered loudly, shaking her by the shoulder. 'Grandmama!'

Grandmama awoke with a start.

'Edmund's collapsed. He's running a fever.'

Grandmama blinked, as if she couldn't quite take in what Amelia was saying. 'Edmund?' she said in wondering voice.

'I'm going down to Kavanagh's pub to get Papa and send him for the doctor,' Amelia went on. 'Do you think Dr Mitchell will come out so late?'

Grandmama was wide awake now. 'Of course he will, child,' she said. 'It's an emergency. He's been our doctor and friend for years.'

'I don't know if there's money to pay him.'

'He won't want paying immediately. We'll pay him when we can.'

Grandmama was already on her feet, ready to go upstairs to Edmund. 'Hurry back, Amelia,' she said. 'I'll be worried about you out on the streets so late.'

Amelia didn't give herself time to worry about being out on the streets at night. There were surprisingly many people about, gathered in laughing groups under gas-lamps and behaving quite differently from the daytime inhabitants of the streets, who always seemed to be in a hurry somewhere. She broke into a trot as soon as she reached the main road, and she kept up the pace until she came in sight of the pub.

It was a warm night, though the summer hadn't quite arrived yet, and the pub door was open to the street. A square of light fell onto the pavement from inside the pub, and shadows moved constantly across the field of light, like a magic lantern show. Laughing voices and loud hulloos reached Amelia's ears from the pub, and as she approached the door she was assailed by a stench of beer and tobacco. The air was blue with smoke and thick with noise and smells. She felt foolish standing there, shifting from foot to foot, wondering how she was going to find Papa in that loud mêlée and imagining herself shouldering her way through the laughing, half-drunken men, peering around for a glimpse of him in the murky light. Just as she was preparing to plunge into the smelly, noisy public house, one of the customers caught sight of her.

'And who have we here?' he called to her, not unkindly, over the heads of his companions.

'Amelia Pim,' she replied from where she stood in the doorway, taking his question literally.

'I see,' he said with a smile. 'And who is Amelia Pim looking for?'

'My father,' she answered gratefully. He could so easily have used the occasion to tease and embarrass her.

Her friend inside the pub looked all around. Then he raised his voice to the rafters and sang out: 'Young lady for Charlie Pim!'

A surge of laughter went up at this, and Amelia blushed, but she stood her ground, and presently a knot of drinkers opened and disgorged Papa, almost at her feet.

He knew immediately he saw her that something was up. 'What is it, Amelia?' he said.

She knew by his voice he hadn't been drinking long. Thank God, she thought.

'It's Edmund, Papa, he needs a doctor. Can you go for him?'

'Edmund!' There was a strange crack in Papa's voice. 'Oh my God! What is it, Amelia? What's wrong with him?'

'I don't know. Oh hurry, Papa. He's very ill. I don't think he's conscious.'

'Just a minute, Amelia,' said Papa, and disappeared back into the browny-yellow maw of the pub. Now what was going on? The seconds ticked by, and Amelia shifted from one foot to the other uneasily. She had lost sight of Papa as soon as he went back into the pub, strain as she would to see him. Her friend who had called her father for her caught her eye again and winked at her. But it was a friendly wink. To her own astonishment, and in spite of her worried state, Amelia winked back.

Just then she started at a clip-clopping sound behind her.

She turned to see Papa atop a spanking dog-cart, with a whip in his hand.

'The publican was just back from some business in town,' Papa called down to her as he turned towards Rathmines, where the doctor lived. 'He hadn't even unhitched the horse. I'll get the doc to Edmund as fast as I can, Amelia. You hurry on home now to him. You're a topping little girl, you know.' And with that he was gone, with a crack of the whip and a whirr of the large, elegant wheels.

# The Diagnosis

Amelia hurried home. She found Edmund still half-conscious, with Grandmama bending over him. The oil lamp still burned on the tallboy, and the room was full of its soft light. Edmund's breathing was fast and shallow, and the sound of it seemed to fill Amelia's ears. His face, which had been pale when she left, was bright now with fever, and every now and then he seemed to murmur something that she couldn't quite catch.

'A fire,' said Amelia to Grandmama. 'I'll set a fire here.'

Grandmama knew a fire wasn't necessary. The night was mild. But it would give Amelia something to do.

'Good girl,' she said. 'That's a good idea.'

Grandmama sat on the side of Edmund's bed and whispered to him while Amelia toiled up and down the stairs with buckets. Amelia couldn't hear what she was saying, but it seemed to comfort Edmund, because his own disjointed murmuring stopped, and – perhaps she was imagining it – his breathing seemed to become more regular.

At last she had a small fire going in the grate. It smoked and spat, but Amelia knew it was only a matter of time before it took off and lit up properly. Then it would be like a friend for Edmund in the room.

When she had taken the fuel bucket downstairs again,

Amelia came back up and joined Grandmama on the other side of Edmund's bed. Now that she had stopped rustling and clanking, she could hear what Grandmama was saying: she was repeating the Lord's Prayer over and over again. After a moment, Amelia joined in: 'Our Father, Which art in heaven, Hallow'd be Thy name ...'

Before they got to 'As we forgive them ...' Amelia heard the patter and the clatter of the dog-cart outside, and Papa's loud 'Whoa, there, boy' to the publican's horse, and the sharp clicking of horse-shoes on the road, as the horse slowed down suddenly. Presently there was the sound of Papa's key in the door and then the two men came pounding up the stairs.

Amelia had always liked Dr Mitchell, but she had never been so glad to see him as tonight. He was tall and terribly thin, which made him seem taller still, and he bent his head as he entered the room, a precaution he always took in strange houses, in case the door lintel wasn't as high as he was.

Grandmama and Amelia excused themselves, partly to allow the doctor to examine Edmund in peace, but mainly because there wasn't enough room for them all in the tiny bedroom.

'You go too, Charles,' said the doctor to Papa, who was staring distractedly at the little heap in the bed that was his son. 'I'll make progress quicker on my own.' The doctor was already poking in his black bag for his stethoscope and his mercury thermometer.

'Can I bring you anything, Doctor?' asked Amelia. She hoped there would be something – hot water, towels, a kettle, a basin – she could be getting. It was dreadful to feel helpless.

But the doctor shook his head. 'Just leave me with him for a few minutes. A little peace is the best thing, now. Make your father a cup of tea, Amelia.'

'Oh yes!' cried Amelia, delighted to be given a task. And she skipped down the stairs ahead of Papa and Grandmama, who lurched down together arm in arm, though there really wasn't room on the narrow staircase.

Papa and Grandmama sat in silence at either end of the kitchen table, while Amelia busied herself making tea. She put out four cups and saucers – everyone might as well have a cup. And this time, she never thought even for a fleeting second of the incident in Findlater's shop as she made the tea. All her thoughts were upstairs by Edmund's bedside.

Or rather not quite all her thoughts. With a little corner of her mind she thought about Mama, and she heartily wished she were here. Grandmama was too silent to be of any comfort to Amelia, and Papa – well, much as she loved her papa, somehow having him there didn't feel like having a grown-up in the house at all.

The doctor came heavily down the stairs, mopping his forehead with a large check handkerchief. It must have been very warm in Edmund's room with the fire lighting, and then there had been so many people.

He drew out a chair and sat down gravely at the kitchen table.

'Dear Lord,' Amelia thought to herself. 'Dear Lord, don't let it be consumption.' Consumption was the worst thing she had ever heard of. She knew it got you in the chest, and Edmund had always been chesty. 'Dear Lord, please, I'll go to Meeting every Sunday and I'll wear any old dresses, just don't let it be consumption.' Then she thought again. She might as well get value for such a big promise. 'Or scarlet fever, or diphtheria, or the croup.' She was adding as many serious illnesses as she could think of.

'Well, Charles,' said the doctor at last. 'I'm afraid it's a bad case of pneumonia.'

Pneumonia! She hadn't thought of that one. If she'd added

that one quickly enough, would she have been able to save Edmund with her prayer? No, that was silly, she realised as soon as she thought it.

'What's the prognosis, Hubert?'

'Well, he's not a strong boy, as you know,' said the doctor slowly. Oh quickly, quickly, say he's going to be all right. 'But he may pull through, with good nursing.'

'Should we move him to hospital?'

'No. I wouldn't recommend it. If he is well looked after here he'll be as well off. The journey wouldn't do him any good, in his present condition. Can you promise me he will be well nursed? Where's Roberta?'

Amelia's mouth fell open. Papa couldn't lie, not in front of Grandmama. If he did, she would simply contradict him. But surely he couldn't tell the truth either. It was too humiliating. Amelia forgot all about being proud of Mama. At that moment, she wished to goodness Mama had never heard of votes for women.

'She's been called away,' said Papa. 'Suddenly. She can't be with us just now.'

Brilliant! Even Grandmama couldn't baulk at that.

'Surely she can come back? In the circumstances.'

'No,' said Papa firmly, making it quite clear he wasn't going to explain or argue. 'Not even in the circumstances.'

'Oh dear. Well, in that case, maybe we should move the lad to hospital after all.'

'No!' thundered Papa. 'Not if there is the smallest risk attached. Amelia will nurse him. I have the utmost confidence in Amelia.'

In spite of herself, Amelia swelled up inwardly. Papa had the utmost confidence in her.

The doctor looked at Amelia. She drew herself up under his gaze and pushed her chin out as if to say, I'll do it! I'll make him well if it's humanly possible.

The doctor rubbed his chin. Then he took out a notebook and wrote down a series of instructions for Amelia. He gave her a thermometer and showed her how to read it. He gave lengthy directions about the preparation of poultices. And he gave her a large bottle of pink medicine, nearly as big as a soda syphon, and he told her to give him a tablespoonful three times a day. He told her what he should drink and how often he should drink. He gave her stuff to rub on his back and stuff to rub on his chest and he asked her if she knew how to make beef tea. She nodded, even though she didn't, because she was sure it would be in Mrs Beeton's book of recipes and advice on household management that Mama kept at all times on the kitchen dresser.

At last he stood up and went to the door. Amelia's heart sank as she watched him go. Now Edmund was her responsibility. At the door the doctor turned and said, 'I'll be back in the morning.' Relief flooded through Amelia.

'Come along, Charles. You'll have to drive me home, as you wouldn't let me take my own horse because you were in such a rush to get me here.'

Grandmama wanted to sit up with Amelia, but Amelia argued that there was no point in both of them losing a night's sleep. She would need Grandmama to take over in the morning. So, reluctantly, Grandmama went to bed. Amelia undressed and put on her dressing-gown, but she didn't go to bed. She sat by Edmund's bed in Mama's old rocking chair, one of the few pieces of furniture they had brought with them from Kenilworth Square, and rocked and listened to the pattern of his breathing. It was an armless rocking chair, the kind called a nursing chair, designed for mothers to sit in and nurse their babies without being hampered by arms. Mama had nursed her and Edmund in it.

Amelia was to bathe Edmund's face every hour with tepid

water, and to give him a drink if he woke. Barley water, the doctor had said, but for tonight plain boiled water would have to do. She sat tensely, listening for any change in his breathing.

Papa came back shortly and joined Amelia. He sat on the foot of the bed with a loud creak and leant sidewards against the bedstead. He was tired. He'd driven to and from the doctor's, four journeys in all, and then he'd had to stable the publican's horse and groom him, and walk home from the pub. He let out a long sigh.

'Oh, Amelia,' he whispered. 'What is to become of us? I wish your mother were here. Poor Edmund.' At this point he beat his fist softly but with feeling on the bedpost. 'Oh God! My little boy! My only son! Don't take away my only son!'

Papa's eyes were tightly closed, but a tear crept down his cheek all the same.

'Oh, Papa,' said Amelia. 'You've got a daughter too.'

She didn't mean that she could ever take Edmund's place. She only said it to comfort Papa, but he must have taken her up wrongly, because he said, 'Ah, a daughter. Daughters are well and fine, but what is a man without a son?'

It was as if someone had hit Amelia in the stomach. Hard. She knew Papa was tired and distraught but even so, whatever did he mean? What was a man without a son? Could it be that Edmund was more to Papa than just Edmund? Could he mean that Edmund was not just his darling child that he couldn't bear to lose, but that he had some sort of special value, because he was a boy? How could that be? Did fathers, for all their doting on their daughters, secretly esteem their sons more highly? Try as she would to excuse Papa, Amelia could not avoid this conclusion. Edmund was more to him than she was, because he was a male child.

Then she felt angry. Not jealous. How could she be jealous of this poor, ailing child she had been put in charge of? How could she feel anything but love and pity for him, who was so weak and so in need of her care? She felt angry. But she wasn't angry with Papa. Papa didn't mean to hurt her, she knew that. He was only saying what was true. That boys were more valuable than girls. That was what made her angry. That bare fact.

Now she thought she had an inkling of what it was that made Mama what she was. Mama must have felt this anger too. It must be this anger that made her walk the streets with a placard and land herself in gaol. At last, Amelia began to understand.

# The Crisis

The next day they moved Edmund into Grandmama's bed, so that Amelia wouldn't have to sleep in a chair in order to be with him at night, and Grandmama took over Edmund's room. Grandmama wanted to take turns in nursing Edmund at night, but Amelia wouldn't hear of it. Grandmama was an old lady. The strain might be too much for her. In any case if something terrible happened to Grandmama in the middle of the night, what use would she be to Edmund? And of course Papa couldn't be expected to keep watch through the night. He had to get up in the mornings to go to work.

For nine days and nine nights Amelia nursed her little brother. At night she slept fitfully, waking hourly to bathe him down and to administer medicines and treatments as the doctor prescribed. Twice in the night she would refill his hot-water jar. During that time, Amelia got to know the hours of the night the way most people know the hours of the day. She knew the darkest hours and when they came, and she knew when the grey streaks in the sky heralded the dawn, and how long it would be before the sun came up. She knew when to expect the birdsong, and when it would be at its most vociferous, and she knew when to expect the cheerful clatter of the milk-cart on the street and the first sounds of the waking city. And as each day dawned, Amelia thought of Mama locked up in her cell in Mountjoy, and she wondered if Mama had a window, and if she was waking up now and seeing the grey light of dawn through the bars. It was almost two weeks since they had seen Mama, and Amelia missed her dreadfully.

In the daytime, Amelia would sleep when she got a chance, to make up for her broken nights. She didn't mind leaving Grandmama in charge of Edmund for a few hours during the day. She napped in Edmund's proper bed, where Grandmama slept at night now.

They let the house go to pot. Grandmama and Papa managed as best they could, scratching meals together and washing up and sweeping and keeping the fire in the range going, but the house was never dusted, the windows were never cleaned, the pots were never properly scrubbed. Nine days is not a very long time, but it is surprising how grimy a house can get in that time, particularly a house in which fires are kept constantly burning. Every time Amelia noticed the dust and dirt, she thought of Mama. For all her madcap ways, Mama would never let the house get like this, and Amelia silently apologised to her.

Every day Amelia changed Edmund's sheets, which were drenched with sweat. Grandmama was too frail to wash clothes, and Amelia was too busy, so they sent everything to the laundry. Grandmama staggered off most mornings with a laundry-bag full of Edmund's bedlinen and she trotted home with the previous day's sheets in a nice tidy parcel, all starched and crisp from the laundresses' hands. The Magdalen Laundry it was called. People said that was where the 'fallen women' worked. Whatever fallen women were, thought Amelia, they were certainly a dab hand with an iron. Amelia sent a load of Papa's shirts there too when he began to complain that he was running out.

Dr Mitchell came daily to check on Edmund. He told

Amelia that she was doing a fine job, better than any hospital nurse. He took off his stethoscope and put it over Amelia's head and showed her how to listen to the heartbeat and how to detect the sound of something wrong in the chest. Amelia was fascinated, but she didn't practise too much with it, because she worried that Edmund would catch cold lying there with his nightshirt up around his neck and his little white body exposed to the air.

'Maybe we'll make a nurse of you, Amelia,' said the doctor cheerfully.

'Oh no,' said Amelia. 'I don't want to be a nurse. I'd like to be a doctor.'

It was only as the words dropped from her lips that Amelia realised that this was her ambition. She turned the idea over in her mind: Dr Amelia Pim, with a bulging little black budget, a stethoscope around her neck and a stopwatch in her pocket. Perhaps she could specialise in looking after children, or maybe in looking after women in child-birth. But definitely she would prefer to be a doctor than a nurse. Nurses did an important job in looking after their patients, but Amelia wanted not just to nurse but to *know*. She wanted to know what made people ill and she wanted to know how to cure them. She wanted to be the one who detected what it was that a patient had, and who decided which were the right medicines, and she wanted to know how to write complicated Latin squiggles for the chemist to decipher.

'Indeed!' said Dr Mitchell with a loud laugh, as if Amelia had made a great joke. 'I think you'll find, Amelia, that a lady can't be a doctor.'

'Why is that, Doctor?' asked Amelia, puzzled.

'Well,' said the doctor, and paused for a moment, as if he couldn't quite think why. 'I suppose,' he said at last, rather lamely, 'it's just not the sort of thing ladies are good at.'

'Oh!' said Amelia, disappointed to have her dream shattered before it had even been properly dreamt.

'Nursing, now,' the doctor was saying, 'that is an honourable profession for a girl with a medical turn of mind. I have known some very fine nurses in my time, excellent women all.'

But Amelia said nothing at all.

On the ninth day, a Saturday, the doctor explained to Amelia that this was the crisis point. That meant that it was an important stage in the development of the pneumonia. If Edmund survived this night, he said, he would pull through.

Amelia wasn't sure whether she was glad or sorry to hear this. Every day up to now, she had been thinking only of the demands of the moment: did Edmund need a drink, was his temperature creeping up, was he in a draught? But now for the first time she began to think about Edmund's dying. No, she mustn't let him die. What if Mama came home from prison to find that Amelia had let her little boy die? It was too dreadful even to imagine.

She wouldn't go to bed at all this night, she resolved. She would keep him alive by sheer will-power.

Sure enough, as the doctor had predicted, the fever seemed to reach a peak that night. The child's eyes rolled in his head, he babbled incoherently, his breath rattled in his throat, and all night, sweat ran in beads off his body and drenched the sheets. All night Amelia sat by him. She tried to force him into consciousness, talking him out of his delirium by keeping up a steady flow of sensible talk, not letting him slip into incoherence. She felt that if she could prevent his mind from rambling, she would somehow save him. She had never thought about death before, but tonight she became convinced it was a breakdown in order and coherence, a descent into chaos and nonsense.

'Mama!' Edmund cried at intervals, reaching his arms up to Amelia.

'No, Edmund. It's Amelia. Mama is away. She will come soon, but not now. This is Amelia speaking, Edmund. Amelia.'

'Mama,' the boy muttered.

'Amelia,' she said firmly.

His lips moved. Amelia put her ear close to hear him.

'Mealy,' he whispered.

'Oh, Edmund!' said Amelia softly. She'd got through to him. He knew her. He was sensible. He was going to be all right.

She looked up and saw the familiar grey streaks pushing through the black of night, and she knew the sun would soon be up. It had been the longest night of her life, and she was thoroughly exhausted. But she had pulled Edmund from the edge of death, and now he was going to live and get well and strong and he was going to be there, up and about, when Mama came home.

Already Edmund's temperature, which had soared in the night, was beginning to come down a little. His cheeks were flaming, but the perspiration in which he had been bathed had halted, and at last his eyes closed in a proper, even sleep.

Amelia went and woke Grandmama and asked her to take over. As soon as Grandmama vacated Edmund's old bed, Amelia sank onto it, fully dressed, and slept her first sound sleep for over a week. She didn't hear Grandmama going to the door to have the milk-can filled when the milk-cart came around or, later in the morning, the solemn peal of the church bells and the families going off to church – children calling out for attention in their Sunday best – on foot, or in carts, one or two adventurous souls on bicycles; she didn't hear the families coming back from church, some of them meeting the congregation of the next mass as they returned, and stopping for a leisurely gossip on the pavement; she never saw the sun rise higher and higher in the sky or smelt the smells up and down the street of Sunday dinners being cooked.

It was lunchtime when she woke, with a bad taste in her mouth and a shivery feeling from having slept over the clothes instead of under them. She still felt tired, but better. She stretched a long stretch and she sighed a long sigh, and then she stood up and went in to see how Edmund had passed the rest of the night. Grandmama had gone to Meeting and left Papa in charge. He sat by Edmund's bed, reading the Sunday newspaper. Edmund was still sleeping deeply, as Amelia had last seen him at five o'clock that morning.

Papa smiled at his daughter. 'He's much better, Amelia,' he said. 'He's going to be all right, isn't he?'

Amelia nodded and smiled back. Then she left the room, closing the door softly, and went downstairs, her heart singing, to get a jug of water to wash in.

As she was washing, Amelia heard the clamour in the street of the people returning from the last mass. It must be lunchtime, she thought. Sunday lunchtime. Good heavens! She was supposed to meet Mary Ann today at the Metropole at two o'clock. Oh dear! She tiptoed back into her own room, where Edmund still slept soundly under Papa's watchful eye, to find something respectable to wear. Amelia scrabbled in the wardrobe. All her nicest dresses had got too short and tight. She'd have to make do with an everyday dress, even though it was Sunday and a special occasion.

'Papa,' she said, as she pulled out first one dress and then another. 'I'm going out for a little while. Will you be all right with Edmund? I'm sure Grandmama will be back shortly.'

She fully expected Papa to ask where she was going, and with whom, and when she would be back. But he just smiled at her again. 'We'll be all right, princess,' he said. 'You deserve a little time off. Enjoy yourself.'

He had spoken to her as if she were a grown-up. Amelia

wasn't sure if she liked that, but just this afternoon, it suited her purposes very well. She didn't want to have to explain about meeting Mary Ann, but equally she didn't want to have to tell a lie. She changed quickly and pulled a brush through her hair, glancing in the mirror as she did so. She was pale, and there were black rings under her eyes. She looked a sight. It struck her, as she reviewed her reflection, that she hadn't looked in a looking-glass for nine whole days.

# The Meeting

Amelia had never seen Mary Ann in her outdoor things before. She looked much older in a coat and hat, but Amelia could see that under the coat she was still as thin as a rake. The two girls viewed each other shyly. Amelia wasn't sure whether to hug Mary Ann or to shake her hand. In the end she did neither, just fiddled with her gloves and smiled at her.

'Well, let's get a move on then,' said Mary Ann at last, settling her heavy basket on her arm. 'I haven't got much time. We can talk as we walk.'

'Where are we going, Mary Ann?' asked Amelia, trotting along beside her friend, who was taking long quick steps and had a look on her face that meant she knew where she was going and intended to get there quickly.

'To London, to see the queen,' said Mary Ann impishly.

'What!' Amelia stopped in her tracks and forced Mary Ann to stop too, pulling at her brown gabardine elbow. 'What are you talking about?'

'Didn't you know the queen was my aunt?' said Mary Ann. 'She's giving a coming-out party for me next week, and I just have to settle the last details about the invitations.'

Amelia had forgotten that Mary Ann's sense of humour could be a bit alarming at times.

'Oh, Mary Ann,' she said wearily. 'Don't play tricks on me, not today. I'm just not up to it.'

'Why?' said Mary Ann. 'Does coming down in the world not agree with you?'

'Oh Mary Ann!' said Amelia, cut to the quick. 'I thought you were my friend.'

'Friend, is it? Some friend you've been, Amelia Pim! I don't hear from you for weeks on end, and then out of the blue there's a telephone call putting the heart crossways in me, telling me my ma was poorly, and now you expect me to be full of smiles?'

'But, Mary Ann!' Amelia was close to tears. Here was her one friend in the world, as she thought, being just as unkind as the rest of them. 'I didn't know where you were. And I was waiting to hear from *you*.'

'But how would I know where you were? You didn't leave me your new address.'

'You didn't leave me yours either.'

'But your ma knew where I was. She got me the job. All you had to do was ask her.'

'My mother ... my mother's away, Mary Ann,' said Amelia softly, her voice almost breaking. 'She's ... she's in gaol, actually.'

'Amelia! Mrs Pim in gaol! Oh lawny!' Mary Ann's shoulders slumped, and she forgot all about her quarrel with Amelia. She set her basket down in the street, as if to concentrate on this piece of news. 'What happened to her?' she asked in disbelief.

'She didn't do anything bad,' said Amelia quickly.

'You don't have to,' agreed Mary Ann. 'Our Pat didn't do anything bad either.'

No, but he might have if he got half a chance, Amelia thought to herself, but she didn't voice this thought. She didn't want to lose Mary Ann's sympathy again.

'Come on, Amelia,' said Mary Ann briskly, picking up her basket again. 'We're going to have to have a little chat, you and me.' And off she set again at a canter.

After a hot and tiring few minutes, they reached Mountjoy Square. The gate to the park in the centre of the square was open, swinging on rusty hinges, and the girls creaked their way in and found themselves a bench in the sunshine. The dark green paint on the seat was blistering, and there was a smell of creosote or oil, but it was pleasantly warm sitting on the weather-beaten wood, and the two girls sat for a moment, their small white faces turned to the sun, which neither of them had seen properly for some time. Mary Ann tucked her basket under the wooden seat, where it was cooler, and she turned to look at Amelia.

'Now,' she said, 'out with it. What's been happening?'

It was as if a dam had burst. All Amelia's terrible experiences of the past weeks came gushing out in a terrific torrent. It was such a relief to tell somebody the whole story: how nasty the girls at school had been to her, then how Mama had been taken away, how Papa had been less than heroic, and how Amelia had felt so depended upon and responsible for everything, with Mama away, and Grandmama old and rather distant most of the time, and Papa distracted by his own sense of failure, Mama's imprisonment, and finally how Edmund had been so ill and Amelia had had to nurse him. Loyally, she drew the line at mentioning Papa's new interest in beer and public houses. 'It's just been one thing after another, Mary Ann,' she finished.

'So it has,' said Mary Ann, in a sympathetic but very matter-of-fact tone. She didn't seem to think the story, disaster-laden as it was, so very incredible as it sounded to Amelia's own ears, even though she had lived through it all. 'But that's the way things always happen, Amelia, one after another.' And she gave Amelia a wink and a smile.

Amelia was so grateful for that wink and smile. It was just like old times. Mary Ann hadn't lost her special gift for taking Amelia out of herself. She sat very still, shoulder to shoulder with her friend, and said nothing for a little while, just enjoyed sitting there in the sunshine with her. A blackbird high in a tree opened his throat and let out a long liquid trill, and a small boy wearing a makeshift triangular sun-hat folded from newspaper trailed along with his head cocked on one side, as if he wanted to scan the ground for interesting things like lollipop sticks or pebbles, but was afraid of losing his headgear.

'Well, it seems to me, Amelia,' said Mary Ann at last, 'that you've done a lot of growing up since I saw you last.'

Amelia glowed.

'Families!' Mary Ann went on, sounding just like a married woman with more children than she could manage. 'They're such a responsibility!'

Amelia gave a little giggle at this parody of womanhood. Yes, there was no doubt that half-an-hour of Mary Ann was exactly what she needed.

'Which reminds me,' said Mary Ann. 'I have my own responsibilities to see to. I'm going to have to go, Amelia.'

The blood drained from Amelia's face. 'No!' she yelped. She couldn't be parted from Mary Ann just yet. She'd only just found her again.

'I have to see my family, Amelia. This is my only day off. I must go.'

'But you haven't even told me about your new position yet,' Amelia protested. Still, she didn't want to be selfish. She knew Mary Ann would have to go. A thought struck her like a flash: 'Can I come with you?'

'Oh, I don't think so,' said Mary Ann, standing up and retrieving her basket. 'It's no place for the likes of you, Amelia.'

'What do you mean, Mary Ann?' Amelia was indignant suddenly.

'I don't mean to be unkind, Amelia. It's just that you're used to better things. You're a young lady.'

'No!' cried Amelia. 'I'm just a ... well, a girl really, a girl like yourself, Mary Ann.' She surprised herself by saying that, but what surprised her was not so much that she made such a claim, but that she didn't give a fig any more for all that young lady nonsense.

Mary Ann looked dubious.

'I insist, Mary Ann,' said Amelia imperiously, unconsciously sounding more young-ladyish than she had all afternoon.

The incongruity of Amelia's tone made Mary Ann laugh. 'Oh well, come on then,' she said.


Mary Ann's family lived all together in one room in a large, old, crumbling house with damp patches on the walls. Amelia got a shock when she went in the front door, which stood permanently open, because so many families used it. The hallway stank, and she had to hold her breath as they climbed the bare stairs. When they reached the Maloneys' room, she was able to let out her breath, because here the air was fresher, mainly because two panes of glass had fallen out and hadn't been replaced, and a breeze constantly blew in. Even so, there was still a strong underlying smell of cabbage, urine and rotting wood – the smell of poverty.

Amelia had never seen so many children in one room before, other than in a classroom. She could hardly believe they were all brothers and sisters. They all seemed to be the same age, for a start, and they were all desperately thin, like Mary Ann. None of them wore shoes, and they all had on an odd assortment of old clothes that had obviously started life in somebody else's wardrobe. Even some of the boys wore skirts. The children swarmed and squirmed everywhere, over chairs and under tables, and a row of them sat on the room's only bed, a large double one, which slouched in a corner, looking as if it had seen better days. The only adult in the room was a middle-aged man, in a coat and hat, who sat at the table, reading an out-of-date newspaper.

'How'ya, Da,' said Mary Ann to the man, taking off her hat and putting it on the oilcloth-covered table.

Immediately a dozen children, or so it seemed, fell upon the hat and squabbled over it, first one trying it on, and then the next snatching it off the first one's head and prancing about with it.

'If you make a mess of my hat, there'll be no tea for any of yous!' warned Mary Ann, who was unpacking the basket she had been carrying.

The children just laughed and continued to pass the hat from one head to the next.

'This is Miss Amelia Pim, Da,' said Mary Ann, laying out a glass jar of potted meat, a cold semolina pudding, partly eaten, two heels of shop-loaf and a quarter of a cake of soda bread, an apple, a ramekin of butter, a small packet of tea, half a bag of sugar, two slices of rhubarb tart, a box of Galtee cheese, a jar of Lamb's plum jam, partly eaten, two hard-boiled eggs, three slices of cooked ham, a bowl of congealed yellow custard and half-a-dozen cold sausages. Finally she produced from her basket a tin can with a lid, presumably full of milk, which she stood carefully on the table, and the carcase of a roasted chicken, totally stripped of meat. 'She's a friend of mine.'

'Humph!' said Mary Ann's father, without removing his hat, but giving it an absent-minded little tip with his index finger. Amelia wondered why he wore it indoors. Maybe he felt the cold, with the glass missing from the windows, even though the day was warm, or maybe he knew that if he put it down, the children would run off with it.

'Sit down, Amelia,' said Mary Ann, pointing to a rickety chair that looked as if it wouldn't take her weight. She sat down gingerly on it, and it creaked in protest, but it didn't crack. Immediately, children started to pull at her skirts and tried to prise themselves up onto her knee. Amelia held herself stiffly, as if she were being over-run by rats. She didn't like small children with snotty noses.

'And how's my little Jimmy?' said Mary Ann, scooping up what appeared to be the youngest and snottiest child, and kissing the top of his head with vigour.

The small fellow squealed with delight as Mary Ann swung him in the air, and Amelia closed her eyes for a moment.

When she opened them again, Mary Ann had plonked the child down on the bed and was pouring water from a bucket into a saucepan over the chicken bones. 'Chicken soup in an hour!' she cried, and the children all clapped their hands.

Amelia didn't ask where Mary Ann had got all the food, but she didn't expect she'd been given it. Stealing, that was called. Amelia looked at these ragged children. Her heart didn't warm to them – she wasn't that sort of girl. But she could see how very thin they were, and she could imagine how hungry they must be. And she knew they were Mary Ann's brothers and sisters, and that Mary Ann must love them.

So was it wrong of Mary Ann to snitch this food for them? she wondered to herself. After all, most of this food was clearly leftovers. It could easily have been thrown out. Obviously it was better to save it for some hungry children than to feed it to the cat or throw it in the bin. The rich family Mary Ann worked for wouldn't miss it. Maybe stealing didn't count if the person stolen from wouldn't miss it. If they wouldn't miss it, then they didn't need it, she argued, and maybe they didn't deserve it in the first place.

Mary Ann cut the bread up into small thin slices, and buttered each slice carefully. Then she spread potted meat on some slices, and she laid pieces of ham on others. She split the sausages down the middle, and laid them on the remaining slices of bread. She peeled the hard-boiled eggs and sliced them thinly and put the slices in a saucer, and she took the cheese out of its box, unwrapped it, sliced it and put the slices on another saucer. She put the jam away for another day. When the chicken broth was ready, she doled it out into cups, mugs, jam-jars, anything she could find, and then she called the children to the table. They all stood around, blessed themselves at a signal from Mary Ann, and sang out together: 'Bless us, oh Lord, and these Thy gifts, which of Thy bounty we are about to receive, AMEN.' And then they fell upon the stolen goodies. Mary Ann was like a referee at a football match, making sure nobody ate more than their fair share. When every last crumb was gone, she spooned out helpings of semolina and custard, and performed the miracle of the loaves and fishes with the two slices of tart, and while they ate that she washed the cups and jamjars, and made tea. Even the littlest children drank tea, well milked.

Mary Ann herself didn't eat, and she didn't offer Amelia anything.

'Well,' said Mary Ann, after they had said goodbye to the Maloneys and were out on the street again, 'that'll be their last decent meal for another fortnight.'

Heavens! thought Amelia, the terribleness of their situation at last coming home to her. That picnic, that scratched-together lunch of scraps and bits, that was their main meal, not only for that day, but for fourteen days! Amelia had thought that the Pims were poor now. But they were rich, overfed, indulged and pampered in comparison to these children. It occurred to her that if one of them got pneumonia, as Edmund had, he would simply die. And suddenly she remembered Mary Ann's mother. Where was she?

'Mary Ann, your mother wasn't there.'

'No,' said Mary Ann briefly.

'She isn't ... she hasn't ...' Amelia was covered in guilt that she hadn't asked Mary Ann about her mother before this. Mary Ann had sat and listened to Amelia's sad story without saying a word about her own family. And if Amelia hadn't insisted on coming, she probably would never have known how bad things were.

'No,' said Mary Ann. 'She's not dead yet. We got her into a home for incurables. That was her wish. She didn't want to infect the young ones.'

Incurables. It had a nasty, defeated sound to it.

'But, Mary Ann, do you ever get to see her?' asked Amelia, shocked.

'No,' said Mary Ann, speaking carefully, as if she were working hard at not crying. 'No. I only have this afternoon off. I can go to her, or I can go to the children. She wants me to go to the children.'

Amelia thought of her own mama and how much she missed her. But her mother would be home soon, and they would all be together then. How could she have been so sorry for herself, when here was her best friend in the world with so much to worry about?

Amelia reached out to Mary Ann and squeezed her wrist. Mary Ann gave her a watery smile.

Amelia and Mary Ann parted on Sackville Street, where they had met. Amelia wanted to make an arrangement to meet again, in a fortnight. But Mary Ann said better not.

'I like you very much, Amelia,' she said. 'And I would like to be your friend. But you see, I have no time for friendship, at the moment.'

'Oh, Mary Ann!' wailed Amelia. 'Don't say that.'

'I'm sorry, Amelia, but there's no point in meeting every other Sunday. You would get weary of my family, and I wouldn't have time to talk to you properly.'

'I wouldn't get weary of it, I promise!' said Amelia hotly, but she knew deep down that Mary Ann was right.

'It's not that I don't want to be your friend, you know. It's just that it can't work. Not just at the moment anyway.'

'Yes, Mary Ann,' Amelia whispered, looking at her boots.

'If you need me badly, you know where to find me, Amelia.'

'Yes, Mary Ann,' said Amelia again. 'Will you at least write to me?'

'Of course I will. Giv'us your address.'

Amelia didn't have any paper, so she repeated her address to Mary Ann.

'Rightio. I've got that now,' said Mary Ann. 'Now, be a big, brave girl, and kiss me goodbye.' She sounded just like a grown-up – a kind aunt, perhaps.

And Amelia Pim, who two months ago thought that she could never be proper friends with a serving girl, put her arms around Mary Ann's thin frame and hugged her hard.

As they drew apart, Mary Ann said: 'Now, Amelia, I want you to give your ma my love, tell her I'm happy in my new situation, and tell her I'm ever so sorry to hear about her bit of trouble. Will you do that?'

Amelia nodded. She would have liked to be able to send her love to Mary Ann's mother, but she didn't know her, and besides, she knew Mary Ann wouldn't be able to get to see her.

'Goodbye, Mary Ann,' she said, her voice almost a whisper.

'Goodbye, pet,' said Mary Ann.

And Amelia stood for a long time, watching the thin little figure tip-tapping smartly up Sackville Street, the empty basket swinging on her arm.

# At the Sign of the Golden Balls

Amelia's birthday dress lay on her bed. She had taken possession of her own bed again, now that Edmund was better, and he had moved back to his room to sleep. During the daytime, he was up and dressed. Every time she looked at Edmund, playing happily with his wooden train or making gingerbread men at the kitchen table and 'helping' with the housework, Amelia congratulated herself and looked forward to Mama's homecoming, which was to be in a few days.

But Amelia didn't want Mama coming home to a big unpaid doctor's bill. Dr Mitchell hadn't actually submitted his bill for attending Edmund, and he wouldn't, because he knew they couldn't possibly pay him for all he had done – coming out late at night, daily visits for nine days, and then more infrequent visits as Edmund made a slow but steady recovery – but Amelia knew that even though the bill hadn't been submitted that didn't mean the money wasn't owed. Amelia wanted that bill paid, before Mama came home.

And so she sat on her bed, fingering her lovely emerald dress and wondering who might want to buy it. Several of the girls at school had admired it immensely on the day of the party, but she couldn't imagine any of them buying a second-hand dress, no matter how pretty it was. Maybe she could put an advertisement in the newspaper, in the Articles for Sale column, but then she'd have prospective customers trailing to the front door, and she definitely couldn't have that. Papa would be so ashamed.

No. She would probably have to settle for whatever a pawnbroker would give her for it, though she knew that was not the way to get full value for it. She suspected it would not be enough to pay Dr Mitchell, but at least it would be a start, and the dress was the only thing of value that she had. She knew she had a bank account, but Papa always made the transactions on her behalf, and she couldn't ask him about it. He wouldn't allow her to use her savings to pay the family bills. Whatever she could get for the dress would simply have to do.

She longed to slip it over her head once again, to hear its friendly chatter as it slid past her ears, as if it were glad to be worn, to feel the skirts billowing and floating under her hands again. It couldn't do any harm, just once, could it? Guiltily, though she didn't know why she should feel guilty about putting on her own dress in her own room, Amelia unbuttoned her everyday pinafore and put on the silk gown. It rustled and whispered, just as she had remembered, and it fell into place about her limbs and body with a sigh of pleasure.

Bristling with anticipation, Amelia turned to look at her reflection. She would look like a princess in her green dress, she knew. Just for a few minutes, she would pretend to be the old Amelia, the rich Amelia who had chosen the stuff for this dress and gone to the dressmaker's in high excitement with her mama for fittings and had glided down the elegant staircase in Kenilworth Square in this very dress, on the day of her thirteenth birthday.

But when she looked, she saw a half-grown, gawky girl whose ears stuck out, her hair streaked with grease from housework, her hands red and lumpy from incessant soakings. Amelia's throat ached as she looked at herself. It wasn't just that her hair needed washing and her hands needed pampering. The old Amelia had simply disappeared: no matter how hard she looked, she couldn't see her. But she still felt like the old Amelia. She still had the same dreams and longings.

Or had she? The old Amelia had thought friends were for inviting to parties and showing off to. The old Amelia had never smelt the stench of poverty. The old Amelia had never nursed a sick child, let alone given the slightest thought to the idea of becoming a doctor. The old Amelia had never felt hurt and angry because boys were considered more important than girls. The old Amelia would have been ashamed, not proud, of Mama.

With a sigh, Amelia changed back into her old dress, and folded up the emerald silk again, laying tissue paper between the folds, and packed it back in its box. The fabric sighed too as she shook it out and folded it away, rustling protestingly, as if it knew her horrid plan. But Amelia didn't listen to it. Firmly, she fitted the lid over the box and marched purposefully downstairs.

It was mid-afternoon. Papa was at the office, Edmund was having his afternoon nap, as the doctor had prescribed until he was completely well, and Grandmama was sewing by the light of the parlour window, working away before the evening started to draw in. Quickly Amelia left the house, and scurried off to Clanbrassil Street, where she knew there were pawnbrokers' shops, or 'money offices' as they genteelly called themselves. She knew you could tell a pawnbroker's by the three golden balls that hung outside, like a promise of new and better worlds within, but she had never been inside one.

She didn't stop to think. That might be fatal. She put her hand on the worn brass handle, smoothed by generations of the hands of the poor, and entered the shop, as the shop-bell clanked. Amelia heard footsteps coming out from the back in response to the bell, and then she heard a voice saying 'Yes?', but she couldn't see anyone.

Where the counter would have been in a normal shop was a huge glass showcase, much taller than Amelia, filled with pocket watches and gold necklets, and lockets containing miniature portraits and little faded locks of hair, and silver teaspoons and snuff-boxes and pill-boxes and tiny gold-threaded evening purses and cufflinks and little gold collar studs and even a silver salt cellar, with a blue glass inset and a tiny salt-spoon, and a shoe-horn with a silver handle. Hanging up all over the shop were men's suits in all shapes and sizes, some complete with shirts and collars, and women's dresses, drooping sadly on hangers, and on shelves all around a raggle-taggle collection of clocks ticked and tocked and chimed and argued, for none of them seemed to tell the same time, and there were teapots, jugs and household items of all descriptions. The shop smelt of mothballs and stale humanity.

Amelia stood on tiptoe, but she still couldn't see the pawnbroker, so she said very loudly, 'I have a silk gown to pledge.' She had no idea where she got the word 'pledge' from, but it seemed to be the right word, because the invisible voice said: 'Well, let's see it.'

Amelia opened the box, and her green dress smiled up at her. At last the pawnbroker came into view. He sidled around the side of the glass case, threw a quick look over Amelia first, in her once-smart coat, and then he eyed the dress disparagingly.

'Five bob,' he said.

'No,' said Amelia, whose throat was dry. She wasn't going to let the dress go that cheaply. 'I want twelve-and-six for it.' She hadn't a clue if that was a reasonable price, but she had quickly doubled the amount he had mentioned and added a bit.

The pawnbroker looked more closely at the dress and felt the stuff.

'Ten shillings is my final offer. Take it or leave it.'

Amelia was just about to say, 'I'll take it,' triumphantly, when she got a sudden rush of courage – after all, there were other pawnbrokers – and instead she said: 'No. I said twelve-and-six and I meant twelve-and-six.'

The pawnbroker fingered his wispy little beard and shook his head. Amelia was just about to put the lid back on the dress, but quite unexpectedly the pawnbroker put out his hand in a gesture that said she shouldn't close the box, and he said 'All right,' and handed her a ticket. Immediately Amelia wished she had said fifteen shillings. For a moment she thought maybe she would chance it. But then she realised this wasn't how you did business in these places. She patted the dress sadly, as if to say goodbye to it, and took the proffered ticket and coins. Then she raced to the door and clanged it behind her, without another word to the pawnbroker. She didn't want to see his thick fingers fumbling at her gorgeous frock.

She headed straight for the little subpost-office around the corner and bought a postal order for twelve shillings and a stamp. Then she went home and wrote a letter to the doctor in her best handwriting:

*Dear Dr. Mitchell*

*Enclosed please find a P.O. in the amount of 12/-, and accept it as a payment on account in respect of your professional services to my brother in his recent illness. If you would be so kind as to furnish an invoice in respect of the outstanding balance of the above-mentioned account, I*

*will give it my best attention at my earliest convenience.*
    *I remain, my dear Dr. Mitchell,*
*Yours faithfully,*
*Amelia Pim*

*P.S.: Edmund is much better now. Thank you ever so much*
*for everything. I think you are a first-rate doctor, but you*
*are wrong about lady doctors and I shall be one some day,*
*you wait and see.*

She had no idea how she was going to give the outstanding balance her best attention at her earliest convenience, but she thought she'd better put that bit in, so the doctor wouldn't think she was trying to get away with just paying a bit of the bill. Then she tucked the pawn ticket under the kitchen clock, and went out to the pillar-box and dropped the letter into it.

And that was the end of her lovely party frock. It was sad, of course, but after all, Amelia wasn't likely to have many opportunities to wear it now that the family lived so much more modestly, and it was better to have no emerald silk dress than to have no Edmund. At that thought, Amelia gave a little shiver, and she pulled her coat around her more tightly as she faced home, even though the air was mild and the trees heavy now with their new foliage. She still had a little change left over, after buying the postal order and the stamp, so she stopped off at a sweetshop and bought a bag of cough lozenges for Edmund – because he liked them rather than because he needed them – and a bag of comforting peppermint humbugs for herself. She popped one into her mouth as she trudged home, and it made a sweet minty lump in her cheek as she went, and altogether the world seemed a better place than it had this time a fortnight ago.

# The Homecoming

Mama was due home on a Sunday afternoon. On the Saturday night Amelia filled up all the pots and kettles that were in the house and set them to boil. She stood the tin bath before the kitchen range and she filled it up with hot water, mixing cold into it until the temperature was just right. Then she bathed Edmund quickly, so that he wouldn't catch cold, using a smooth, translucent bar of Pears soap she used to keep in a china dish on her dressing table in Kenilworth Square. She quickly washed his hair, putting vinegar in the rinsing water to make it gleam, and then she pulled his glistening little body out of the bath, stood him on a towel, wrapped him in another towel, and rubbed his hair with a third towel to get as much of the water out of it as she could. When he was quite dry, even between his toes, she dressed him in a clean nightshirt and then she carefully brushed his hair until it dried in the warm kitchen air and sat like a little gold cap about his pale forehead.

Amelia bundled Edmund off to bed with a hot-water jar and a perfunctory story, and then she had a quick bath herself in the firelight. She washed her own hair too, but it took much longer to dry, and she sat contentedly in the glow of the range, looking at her pink toes, and endlessly brushing her shining mane.

Next day, they all went to early Meeting. It was Edmund's first outing since his illness, and Amelia made sure he had a good nourishing breakfast first, and she buttoned up his coat over the little sailor suit he wore on Sundays. She noticed that the cuffs didn't come down as far as his wrists. He evidently hadn't stopped growing during his spell in bed.

When they were all dressed and ready to go, Papa whisked a surprised Edmund onto his shoulders, saying: 'You may have a ride, at least part of the way, son, but don't jig about or the horse will buck. Come along, Mama!' This last was to Grandmama, who was fussing with her parasol, a remarkably plain parasol, Amelia noticed.

'Duck, boy,' shouted Papa, and Edmund ducked his head just in time not to be smacked in the nose by the door lintel, and with that the Pim family set off at a brisk pace. It was a fine day and the streets looked fresh and bright in the light of morning. It wasn't much above a mile, down Camden Street and South Great George's Street and across Dame Street to Eustace Street, but Papa's shoulders must have ached by the time they got there.

'Why is the Meeting House on such a poky little side-street, Papa?' asked Amelia as they approached it, thinking of Christ Church standing proudly on its little knoll and St Patrick's Cathedral with its spire overlooking the humble buildings around it.

'Penal Laws, Amelia,' said Papa.

'What sort of laws are they Papa?'

'They aren't laws now, Amelia, but they were once upon a time. Only the steeple-houses of the Established Church, which was the Church of Ireland, were allowed to be on the main streets. Papists, Quakers, and Dissenters of all sorts had to skulk in side-streets. Even the Pro-Cathedral, the main Roman Catholic church in Dublin, is on a side-street. There's a Non-Subscribing Presbyterian church on Eustace Street also, whatever a Non-Subscribing Presbyterian might be when he's at home.'

'Are we Dissenters, Papa?'

'Yes, my girl, we most certainly are. We dissented from the Established Church, but that is only the start of it. We dissent from such a great many things, that I couldn't begin to list them.'

'You make us sound querulous, Charles,' said Grandmama, not looking too pleased.

'That's right, Mama,' said Papa with a grin, looking and sounding quite like the old Papa as he strode along in the sunshine with Edmund on his shoulders. 'God's Quarrellers, that's us.'

'That's not fair, Papa,' said Amelia, suddenly serious. 'We are not a quarrelsome people at all. In fact, above all the things we believe in, not quarrelling and fighting is probably one of the biggest things.'

'No, you're right, Amelia,' said Papa, grave too all of a sudden. 'But we are an opinionated people.' Then he grinned again and said: 'But then our opinions are right!'

'Charles!' said Grandmama, but Amelia noticed that she took out her handkerchief and blew her nose with what seemed like unnecessary force, almost as if she were hiding a little snort of laughter.

Amelia couldn't remember when they had all last marched along together like this, poking harmless fun at each other. It must be the thought of Mama coming home that made them all so light-hearted.

Even when they entered the Meeting Room, with its grave brown furniture, looking for all the world like a courtroom, their spirits remained high, and they nodded and smiled to their friends and relations as they took their places and bowed their heads. People leant over and patted Edmund encouragingly on the head, and one or two whispered 'Well done!' to Amelia. They must all have heard how she had worked to save Edmund, and they were congratulating her now. Amelia sat and looked at the pattern which the sunlight coming in at the high-placed windows made on the floor and she felt thankful for Edmund's life, for Mama's home-coming, and for the sunshine. She felt regretful, too, for their old way of life, but her regrets were starting to fade, and already she was finding new things to be glad about in their new life, small things, but still, they were there. Her only major regret was the loss of Mary Ann's companionship. She knew she hadn't lost Mary Ann's friendship, but she missed her presence and her quirky jokes.

Just before the Meeting for Worship began, the Jacob family entered the Meeting Room. Amelia heard loud whispering from Dorothea, her old classmate, whom she hadn't seen since Mama's arrest, and she thought Dorothea must be urging her parents to avoid the Pims. She knew Dorothea mustn't like her, because she had been avoiding her at school since the birthday party. Amelia concentrated on the sunny patterns on the floor and looked neither right nor left. But then, quite unexpectedly, Dorothea clunked into the bench next to Amelia, followed by the rest of her family. 'Hello,' breathed Dorothea in Amelia's ear. Amelia turned and smiled politely, and wondered what was going on.

Amelia amazed herself. She sat still for the whole Meeting and she hardly even noticed. She couldn't in all honesty say that she had been thinking the right kind of Christian thoughts all the time, but she never once fidgeted. When the Meeting drew to a close, the Jacob family stood up to leave immediately. They must have a roast in the oven, thought Amelia enviously. Just as they left, Dorothea seemed to lurch against Amelia, and something small but heavy fell into Amelia's lap.

'Dorothea!' Amelia hissed at her schoolmate's back, as she

felt in the folds of her skirt for whatever it was Dorothea had let fall.

Dorothea turned and put her finger to her lips and shook her head rather too fiercely for somebody who had just attended Meeting. Amelia was puzzled, but didn't say any more. As Dorothea's plump figure disappeared through the door, Amelia's fingers closed over a small, heavy package. It felt somehow familiar as she held it in her hands. Quickly she tugged at the wrapping paper, and out fell a gold watch on a slender gold neck-chain onto her lap. Amelia picked it up. It was the very watch Papa had given Amelia on her birthday and she had lost in the school-yard. Amazed, Amelia stared at the watch. The adult Pims were making low conversation in the aisle with a family they had met, and only Edmund saw as Amelia slipped the watch chain over her head and the watch settled against the front of her dress, as if it had always been there. Edmund looked quizzically at his sister, but Amelia smiled a don't-breathe-a-word signal at him, shaking her head and putting her finger over her lips. Edmund shrugged his shoulders as if to say that older people were very odd and turned away, losing interest already.

All the way home, Amelia felt the weight of the watch around her neck, and every few moments she fingered it, to make sure it was still there. How very odd the episode with Dorothea had been, to be sure.

After lunch, Papa went off to fetch Mama home. He said he would hail a hansom cab on Berkeley Road and bring her home in style. Amelia worried about the cost of the cab, but she said nothing, as of course Mama must come home by carriage. She couldn't be expected to walk, or even to wait for a tram.

While Papa was gone, Amelia and Edmund put the finishing touches to their preparations. Once Edmund had recovered, Amelia and Grandmama had undertaken a big spring-cleaning, dusting and polishing and shining up every corner of the house, room by room. Together they had cleaned all the windows, till they twinkled in the sunlight, and they'd washed down all the paintwork – doors, archi-traves, skirting boards and dado rails. It was only when they did this that Amelia noticed how handsomely the woodwork was made, and how straight and neat all the little grooves and notches were. Really it wasn't such a bad little house after all, not elegant, but certainly not ugly either.

The copper pipes leading to the kitchen sink hadn't been properly boxed in and hidden from view, the way they would be in a more prosperous house, but when Amelia polished them with Brasso and a soft cloth, they gleamed with a pinkish glow that made her heart glad, and when she lit the oil-lamps in the evenings after that, the shining pipes winked at her, as if to thank her for making them so handsome.

She had taken the only rug in the house, the one on the parlour floor, out to the yard and had beaten it mercilessly on the line with a brush handle. That was a filthy job, and when she blew her nose afterwards, her handkerchief was streaked with black dust, and she even had to dig gritty dust from the carpet fibres out of her ears, but it was worth it, because when she laid the carpet down and sponged it over with a mild solution of soap and water, all the reds and blues came gleaming up at her, and the rug positively glowed on the floor after that.

In a tin trunk of Mama's, Amelia had found some lace tablecloths, with patterns of flowers and leaves, hearts and stars, diamonds and birds-of-paradise. She washed them and bleached them and starched them, and she spread some of them on the more disreputable tables that stood about the house looking the worse for wear, and one large one she hung as a drape at the parlour window.

The last lace tablecloth she spread on her parents' bed, over the moth-eaten pink quilt, and it fell gracefully to the floor, the pink of the quilt glowing through its lacy pattern and looking quite unlike its stained and battered self.

She found an old brass cache-pot with round handles like miniature door-knockers in the lean-to shed, all green with age and thick with grime, and she polished that up too and bought a small house plant for it, and stood it on one of her newly washed lace cloths. Now the parlour looked homely and welcoming, especially in the evenings, when the fire was crackling and the lamps were lit and the rug's colours flickered in the firelight. All it needed now was Mama at its centre, reading a book or writing a letter, to make it into a proper family living room.

When at last they heard the key in the door, Edmund and Amelia could hardly contain their excitement. Grandmama didn't seem in the least excited. She sat quietly reading her Bible, not sewing, because it was Sunday.

Edmund and Amelia ran into the little hall to greet Mama, as she came in on Papa's arm. The hall was decked with paper chains and chinese lanterns Edmund had made using coloured crêpe paper and cowgum, just as he had done for Amelia's birthday party, and there was a large banner facing the hall door, saying: 'Well Come Home Mama'. Amelia hadn't corrected the spelling, as she wanted Mama to know Edmund had done it all by himself.

Edmund threw himself at Mama's knees, and she bent down and picked him up, though he was far too big for such babying. As she hugged him close, she looked over his head into Amelia's eyes, and Amelia was shocked at what she saw. Mama had got terribly thin, her eyes were drawn and bloodshot, and her hair, hanging down endearingly on one side as usual was streaked with grey. Had there been grey in it before? Amelia couldn't remember for certain, but she thought not.

At last Mama put Edmund down. He clung to her skirt, but Mama opened her arms to Amelia, and gave her a long, wordless hug. At last she spoke, and her first words were: 'I'm sorry, darling.'

Amelia couldn't speak, but if she could have she would have told Mama not to say that, that she wasn't cross or hurt but proud of her. Instead she just hugged her again.

'Mama! Mama!' Edmund kept squawking. 'Where were you?'

'I was away, Edmund,' said Mama.

'But where, Mama? Where?'

Mama sighed. How could she tell a six-year-old where she had been?

Then Papa spoke up: 'Mama was a guest of the king's, Edmund.'

'Oooh!' squeaked Edmund excitedly. 'Does the king live in a very large house, Mama?'

'Very large,' agreed Mama.

'And has he got a golden crown, Mama?'

'Very golden,' smiled Mama, stroking Edmund's head. 'But not as golden as my little boy's hair.'

And then the family moved together, jostling in the confined space of the tiny hallway, but all holding hands or linking arms, forming an affectionate knot, into their welcoming, smiling little front parlour, and shut the door.

# A Misunderstanding

The very next day, Amelia went back to school, for the first time in over a month. Her wardrobe was in a sorry state by now. Most of her dresses were simply too short or too tight or both. All they were good for now was cutting up for patches for other dresses, or making into dusters and polishing cloths. The few things that did fit her were patched and worn.

The last time Amelia had gone back to school after a family disaster, she had been able to pretend, at least for a while, that nothing very dramatic had happened, but this time, it was clear from just looking at her that there had been a change for the worse in the Pim family fortunes. In any case, Amelia knew from the way people had spoken at Meeting on Sunday that the story of Mama's imprisonment was well known among the Quaker families. So Amelia didn't even try to pretend. When Lucinda Goodbody asked loudly, so everyone could hear, 'And where have you been, Amelia Pim?' as if she didn't know quite well where she had been, Amelia answered quietly: 'I was needed at home, Lucinda. Hadn't you heard?'

That took the wind out of Lucinda's sails. She had been expecting Amelia to try to bluff her way with some story or other, and Lucinda had been determined to call her bluff.

But she didn't quite know how to react when Amelia simply spoke the truth.

'Well,' said Lucinda loudly, regaining her poise after a moment, 'I suppose *somebody* had to keep house while your mama was IN PRISON!' She spoke the last words extra loudly, in case anyone might miss them.

A communal gasp ran around the classroom. Everyone knew, but no-one thought anyone would actually say it out loud. An excited little buzz followed the gasp, and a few people muttered encouraging remarks to Lucinda.

'Exactly, Lucinda,' said Amelia very coolly, though she didn't feel cool at all, but on the contrary very turbulent and warm inside. 'You've put your finger on it. That is exactly the case. When you have a heroine in the family, like my mama, you just have to make some sacrifices. That's the way it is.' And she went on unpacking books from her satchel and not meeting Lucinda's eye. Another little buzz followed this reply of Amelia's. The girls had gathered around now, in a wide circle, to observe the sparring match.

Again, Lucinda was taken aback by Amelia's very simple strategy of agreeing with her. She cast about for something more hurtful to say, to see if she could goad Amelia into a row.

After a moment, she said, to the assembled class: 'Well, girls, I suppose we shall have to welcome her back to the bosom of the class, Miss Amelia Pim. Poor thing, her father is a bankrupt, her mother is a jailbird, and she was seen one Sunday afternoon on Sackville Street in intimate conversation with a *fallen woman*!'

The gasp that flew around the classroom at this last remark was much bigger and more dramatic than the first gasp. All eyes were upon Amelia now, to see how she would react to this.

Perhaps fortunately for Amelia, she had no idea what

Lucinda was talking about, so she was able to look her in the eye and say: 'I don't know any fallen women, Lucinda.'

'You most certainly do, Amelia Pim. You told me yourself your maid was in the family way.'

Amelia looked at Lucinda in great puzzlement. Lucinda must be talking about Mary Ann, but Mary Ann wasn't a fallen woman. As far as Amelia was aware, Mary Ann had never worked in a laundry in her life, and even if she had, what was that to Lucinda? And what had her family got to do with it? Could Lucinda have heard that Mary Ann was pinching food from the Shackletons to feed her starving brothers and sisters? Well, even if she had, Amelia was going to stand up for her friend.

'What's wrong with having a family, Lucinda?' she asked.

Lucinda replied: 'Nothing at all, if you're married.'

There she went again, obsessed with the idea of Mary Ann getting married. The last time Lucinda had brought this subject up, there had been something about Mary Ann not being able to get married because her brother was in gaol. Was Lucinda trying to bring the conversation around to people with family members in prison again?

'Lucinda, you seem to be terribly interested in the marrying habits of other people,' said Amelia grandly. 'Really, one wonders if you aren't a little young to be so interested in that sort of thing.'

This time it was a gasp of admiration that flew around the classroom, followed by a few mild titters.

Lucinda got pink in the face. 'Well,' she said, 'I'm certainly old enough to know that it is not the thing to consort with a servant in the street, especially not a servant in disgrace.'

'Mary Ann is not in disgrace!' exclaimed Amelia.

'Well, she ought to be. She ought to be ashamed of herself, expecting a baby and not even old enough to be married.'

What followed this remark was more than a gasp or a buzz

or a titter, it was a positive roar. Lucinda had gone too far this time. As the excitement died down a little, Dorothea Jacob piped up: 'Really, Lucinda, I don't see that it's any business of yours what people's servants do or don't do, and if Amelia chooses to help out a poor girl in trouble, then I think we should all admire her. Good for you, Amelia!'

'That's right,' murmured another brave soul.

'Well done, Amelia,' said a third.

'Good egg, Amelia!' said someone loudly, and in a moment the girls were crowding around Amelia, smacking her on the back and smiling and welcoming her back.

Amelia didn't really understand what Lucinda had been saying. She didn't know where Lucinda had got the idea that Mary Ann was going to have a baby from, but obviously it was some misunderstanding. Anyway, she wasn't interested in pursuing the silly conversation any further, so she let it drop and she turned a smiling face to the girls who were saying kind things and she replied to their enquiries about Edmund and her mother, and ignored Lucinda for the rest of the morning.

Amelia had to concentrate hard during lessons, in order to catch up on all the schoolwork she had missed out on while she had been absent, so it wasn't until coffee-break that she got a chance to seek Dorothea out.

Dorothea was sitting in a corner, reading a book. Amelia sat down next to her and said quietly: 'Thanks for sticking up for me earlier, Dorothea.'

Dorothea turned a pair of frightened eyes on Amelia, and immediately looked away again, without saying anything.

'And thanks for returning the watch,' added Amelia.

'Oh Amelia,' said Dorothea in a small, tearful voice, still not looking up. 'I didn't mean to steal it. In fact, I didn't really steal it. You dropped it when you were being bumped on your birthday. I just picked it up, and I was about to hand it to you, when something made me not do it. I was feeling so jealous of you with your lovely fair hair and your fine motor-car and your party and your expensive watch. I thought I would just punish you a little, by keeping the watch for a while.'

Amelia nodded and said nothing. At last Dorothea looked at her.

'I told my sister Elizabeth. I thought she would think it a great joke. But she was shocked at what I had done, and insisted on coming to the party with me, to make sure I gave it back. But then I fainted, and then you disappeared, and ... well, then ... I should have given it to you the next day at school, but then you seemed so upset about something, and I didn't like to talk to you, so I thought I wouldn't say anything about it for a little while yet, and then, suddenly, you stopped coming to school.'

'That was when Mama was arrested,' explained Amelia.

Dorothea stopped, embarrassed. Then she said in a low voice: 'Whoever put your mother in prison made a great mistake.'

'Thank you, Dorothea,' Amelia said. And she really was grateful.

'Anyway,' Dorothea went on, 'I was afraid to post the watch, in case it broke. So I just kept it in a little package in my pocket until I saw you again. I was so pleased when you finally came to Meeting on Sunday.'

'Were you?' This was nice to hear, even if the reason was a bit peculiar.

'Oh, yes. You have no idea how dreadful I have felt ever since that day when I took it. Amelia, I'm very sorry.'

Amelia felt old and wise and kind.

'Oh, Dorothea,' she said, 'it's only an old watch. It doesn't matter in the least.'

Of course it had mattered at the time, dreadfully. But

Amelia spoke the truth now when she said it didn't matter in the least. Changed circumstances had changed her view of what mattered.

'I've been longing to tell you for weeks,' said Dorothea. 'I feel much better now. Thanks, Amelia.'

Dorothea looked better too. At least she didn't look like a frightened rabbit any more.

Now that she knew the full story of what had happened to the watch, Amelia felt she could talk about it. She showed the watch to Mama that evening, as they sat companionably in the parlour, after Edmund and Grandmama had both gone to bed, and while Papa was working at some figures in the kitchen, and she told her the whole story.

'Poor old Dorothea!' said Mama.

'What about poor old Amelia?' said Amelia indignantly. How very like Mama, to say such a thing! Amelia felt especially stung, when she considered how prettily she had forgiven Dorothea that afternoon.

'Oh, poor old Amelia, then, too,' conceded Mama. 'I know you were very upset when the watch disappeared. You never said a word, but we did all notice. But somehow I don't think the watch matters to you so much any more.'

And that was just like Mama too, to put into words what Amelia had been trying to think herself.

'And,' said Mama, 'it sounds to me as if you've made yourself a friend in Dorothea. So perhaps losing the watch wasn't such an ill wind after all.'

Amelia thought about this for a while. Dorothea wasn't as pretty or as popular as Lucinda, or as witty as Mary Ann, but she had stuck up for Amelia in a crowd, and she had been brave about the watch. She was quite nice, really, when she wasn't being rabbitty.

'Mama,' said Amelia, after she'd been thinking for a while about what had happened in school that morning.

'What's a fallen woman?'

Mama explained that that was a not very kind expression to mean a woman who had been got into trouble by a man, especially an unmarried woman who had a baby.

'Oh,' said Amelia. 'I thought it meant somebody who worked in a laundry.'

'Amelia!' Mama said with a gasp that turned into a giggle. 'Oh yes, I see now.' And she explained that sometimes poor girls in trouble got taken in by the nuns who ran the laundries, and were given jobs to do to earn their keep.

'Often these girls stay on and work in the laundries for the rest of their lives,' Mama continued, 'long after their babies have grown up. It's a sad business. But why do you ask, Amelia? Who's been talking to you about "fallen women"?'

'It was Lucinda Goodbody, Mama. She keeps calling Mary Ann by that ugly name, and saying she is going to have a baby.'

'What a nasty little mind she must have, to be sure. Where could she have got the idea that our Mary Ann was in the family way?' Mama wondered aloud.

'Oh, Mama!' cried Amelia. 'Is that what being in the family way means? I thought it just meant having a family, you know, being part of a family, like you and Papa and Edmund and Grandmama are my family. Oh Mama, I must have given Lucinda the wrong idea about Mary Ann!' And Amelia clapped her hand over her mouth.

Mama smiled at this, but Amelia was too embarrassed at her dreadful mistake to see the humorous side of it.

'Never mind, Amelia,' said Mama. 'I'm sure Mary Ann won't ever get to hear of it. I don't suppose she is ever likely to meet Lucinda Goodbody socially. I wonder how Mary Ann is getting on in her new position,' she added.

Amelia had been wondering whether to come clean about

the telephone call and the meeting at the Metropole and the visit to Mary Ann's family home. She was a bit worried that Mama might not approve of what she had done. But she did want to pass on Mary Ann's message. So now she told the story of the meeting and how Mary Ann had said they couldn't go on meeting just now because Mary Ann had so many family responsibilities. Finally she told her about Mary Ann's mother.

'Poor old Mary Ann!' said Mama. 'And poor Amelia, too!' she added before Amelia got a chance to pout. 'I didn't realise you had been missing Mary Ann so much. And now you're missing her again!'

'It's not so bad now that I know where she is and we can send each other letters,' said Amelia. 'Hers are very scrawly because she has to write when she's tired, but you can hear her laughing when you read them.'

'I have an idea,' said Mama. She had that gleam in her eye that she got when she saw an opportunity to do good works. 'I'll tell you what, Amelia, we must find out which home Mrs Maloney is in. I'll write to Mary Ann in the morning and find out. I'm sure she would be pleased if we paid her mother a visit, and brought her some fruit or cake. And you can tell her you've been talking to Mary Ann recently, and that she is well. That's the friendliest thing you could possibly do for Mary Ann, because she can't go and visit her mother herself.'

Amelia didn't know if she wanted to go on an errand of mercy to see a strange, dying woman, but she knew Mama wouldn't be deflected, and she knew also that Mama was right – that *was* the best possible thing she could do for Mary Ann.

'Why are some families so very poor, Mama?' she asked, 'when others are so rich?'

'It's not very fair, is it?' said Mama.

'Could it be, Mama, that poor people don't try hard

enough and don't look after their money well and save it? Like Mrs Kelly.'

'Who is Mrs Kelly, Amelia?'

'The woman who was to come and help in the kitchen on the day of my birthday party, Mama. She didn't bother to turn up. How can she expect to get money if she doesn't come and earn it when it is offered to her?'

'Ah, Amelia,' said Mama with a sigh. 'It wasn't that Mrs Kelly didn't turn up. It was I who had to cancel the arrangement. Things had got very bad in Papa's firm by then, and I simply didn't have the spare cash to pay her. We had great difficulty in getting enough money together to finance the party food, not to mind paying extra staff. That's why Mrs Kelly didn't arrive. It had nothing to do with the fecklessness of the poor.'

'Oh dear,' said Amelia, 'I didn't realise.'

'So you see, Amelia,' Mama went on, 'you can't say the poor are to blame for being poor. Any more than you can argue that women are to blame for not having the vote.'

'Oh, Mama, you are incorrigible!' laughed Amelia. 'I will *not* hear a lecture on women's suffrage at this hour of the night.'

'Am I terribly boring about it, Amelia?'

'No, Mama. *It's* a bit boring, I suppose, but *you're* not. You're rather splendid, Mama, going to gaol for your principles and all.'

'And leaving my poor daughter to keep the family going and to nurse a sick child? I don't call that very principled.'

'I didn't mind, Mama, really I didn't. I mean, it was frightening when Edmund was so ill, and I missed you dreadfully and I worried about you. But it was nice to be so ... well, to feel so important, Mama.'

'Well, I think you've been splendid too, Amelia,' said Mama. 'And now it's time for bed.'

Amelia stood up. 'Anyway, it's getting less boring,' she said. 'Your votes for women stuff, I mean.'

'You mean you're beginning to find it interesting,' said Mama.

'Same thing, Mama.'

'Oh no, Amelia,' said Mama, kissing a small secret smile into her daughter's hair. 'Not the same thing at all.'

# The Letter

One morning Amelia received a letter. It was in a thick white square envelope addressed in a strong hand. It sat by Amelia's plate when she came down to breakfast. She didn't often get letters, and she certainly didn't ever get letters from grown-ups. This was sure to be from a grown-up, as the handwriting was so strong and fluent.

She took her knife, which she hadn't yet got butter on, and slit the envelope. Out slid a thick piece of white writing paper, to which was attached, as she saw when she unfolded it, an onion-skin-flimsy smaller square of paper. The flimsy square of paper was printed in copper-plate script, with some parts filled in by hand:


*Rec'd from ... Miss Amelia Pim*
*The sum of ... 0.12s.0d.*
*With thanks*


And it was signed with an indecipherable squiggle.

Amelia lifted the flimsy sheet aside and read the hand-written letter:

*Dear Miss Pim,*

*Please find enclosed a receipt for monies received in respect of professional attendance on Master Edmund Pim. Your prompt settlement of this account is gratefully acknowledged, and I beg to inform you that no further payment is due in respect of this account.*

*With regard to your ambitions for a career in medicine, I have given the matter more consideration, and I wish to advise you that on reflection I have revised my view as expressed on a previous occasion. I am of the opinion that you are already a very fine nurse, and given your determination, intelligence and strength of character, I see no reason why you shouldn't some day make a very fine doctor.*

*If your ambitions are still in the medical line when you reach university age, perhaps you would care to consider a proposition I may be in a position to make with regard to assisting you in the pursuit of your studies.*

*I remain, my dear Miss Pim, with renewed thanks for your prompt settlement of the above-mentioned account,*

*Your very humble servant,*
*Hubert Mitchell*

Amelia could feel her heart beating faster and her face glowing pinkly as she read this letter. When she looked up, all her family's eyes were on her.

'Well?' asked Mama.

'Oh, it's just a letter,' said Amelia.

'Who is it from, Amelia?' pursued Mama.

'A friend,' said Amelia nonchalantly, stuffing it carelessly into her pocket and reaching for a slice of toast.

'Amelia,' said Mama in a firm voice. 'You are too young

to receive secret letters. Either you tell me who the letter is from, or you hand it over.'

'Oh Mama!' whined Amelia, but she knew it was to no avail. Sullenly she fished the letter out of her pocket and handed it over, without looking at Mama. Mama read the letter in silence, and passed it to Papa.

'What is the meaning of this, Amelia?' asked Papa as he read it. 'Please find enclosed ... in respect of professional attendance ... no further payment ...' And he flicked the flimsy square of paper over and examined it. 'This is a receipt, Roberta,' he said in astonishment.

Both her parents fixed their gaze on Amelia.

'I paid the bill. That's all.' She looked over the top of her teacup at them.

'Yes, that much is clear, dear, but where did you get the money?'

There was nothing for it but to tell the story of pawning the dress. Amelia looked steadily at her plate and mumbled her story. 'I got twelve-and-six for it,' she finished, 'so I sent Dr Mitchell twelve shillings and I used the sixpence for the stamp and to get some sweets for me and Edmund.'

'Amelia!' said Papa in a shocked voice.

'Well,' said Amelia defensively, 'it was a long time since we had had sweets.'

But it wasn't the sweets Papa was concerned about. 'You mean to say,' he went on, 'you went into a pawnshop, and you pawned the lovely dress your mama got you for your birthday!'

'Yes, Papa,' Amelia muttered.

'Roberta!' Papa turned to Mama in an appeal for support. He wasn't angry, exactly, but he was very taken aback. 'We can't have our children pawning the clothes off their backs.'

'No, Charles, we can't,' said Mama quietly. 'But a party frock is not exactly the clothes off anyone's back. It is a luxury item. And I don't think we should be remonstrating with our daughter about this, my dear. I think she has made a very brave sacrifice, and I think we should be congratulating her. Do you realise, Charles, how much that dress meant to her?' And Mama turned a pair of shining eyes on Amelia. Amelia felt shy and pleased and confused all at the same time.

But Papa laid his head right down on the kitchen table and gave a long, low moan.

After a moment he looked up and said: 'I'm sorry, Amelia. I didn't mean to appear to criticise you. It is myself I blame, that it should come to this. But I solemnly promise you all that it will never happen again. If I have to kill myself with work, there will be money in this house to pay the bills.' And he stood up as if he could make a little extra by getting to work earlier, and strode out of the room.

After a little while, Amelia said to Mama: 'He didn't even read the important bit.'

'I know,' said Mama with a small smile. 'Perhaps it's just as well. He's feeling a bit touchy just now, and he might think Dr Mitchell was offering charity that he couldn't take. I think we won't mention it just for the moment, Amelia, if you don't mind. And I'm very, very pleased to hear that you are considering becoming a doctor. I have to say that I agree with Dr Mitchell that you would make a very fine one. But not unless you pass all your examinations, and that starts with getting to school on time. Off you trot now!'

Amelia snatched up her satchel and trotted off, just as Mama had ordered, and all the way, she imagined herself in a white coat – a very elegantly cut white coat, of course – sweeping around the wards of a big hospital, glancing at people and pronouncing them well. If she had the least doubt about their being well, she would stop by their bedside and enquire as to their regularity, while holding their wrist aloft in one hand and peering all the while at her gold watch and giving a knowing little sigh as they described their symptoms. Then she would give the nurses a long and complicated list of instructions and the patient some sound advice as to their diet.

# Glad News

After luncheon on the following Sunday, Papa announced that they were all going on a little jaunt. He told Amelia and Edmund to get their outdoor things on smartly. He refused to say where they were going, just that they would have tea out. Amelia was rather concerned to hear this. Sometimes there was hardly enough money for tea *in*. She hoped Papa wasn't becoming extravagant, as he used to be in the old days. She threw a little worried glance in Mama's direction, but Mama was busy doing up Edmund's buttons, and she couldn't catch her eye. She looked at Grandmama, who disapproved of excess, and who disapproved even more of entertainment on a Sunday afternoon, but even Grandmama looked unconcerned, and was fussing with her drab little parasol again.

It seemed as if Papa was looking for ways in which to squander money, for not only were they to indulge in the extravagance of tea out, but, as soon as the little party of Pims reached the main road, Papa hailed a passing cab and bundled them all into it, taking no notice of Amelia's squawking protests. When they were settled in the cab, the ladies and children on the inside, and Papa out of earshot on the seat up beside the cabby, Amelia tried once again to catch Mama's eye.

'Mama,' she said in a fierce whisper. 'This must be costing a small fortune!'

But Mama just gave a secretive half-smile and looked out of the window at the Sunday afternoon families out on walks, children whooping along in front, adults coming sedately behind. Still Grandmama fussed, this time with the buttons of her gloves.

'I always said,' she announced plaintively, to no-one in particular, 'that buttons were an unnecessary nonsense on gloves, and now look, this one's just about to fall off. Should I pull it off completely and put it in my pocket, or do you think it will hold the afternoon?'

Amelia gathered that this last question was directed to her.

'Oh,' she said. 'Goodness me, Grandmama, what did you say?'

But Grandmama just grumbled softly to herself and didn't ask Amelia's opinion again.

They all jostled and rolled as the cab bumped over the cobbled streets, and Amelia was just beginning to get into the rhythm of the horse's stride when they pulled up.

'Botanical Gardens!' shouted the cabby.

'Botanical Gardens!' repeated Papa, opening the door of the cab with a flourish and handing the ladies down.

'What on earth ...?' said Amelia.

'Finest botanical gardens in Europe,' said Papa, herding them all in at the gate, and no-one could contradict him, for they had no idea what botanical gardens were.

But it appeared that Papa was correct, for certainly the gardens were pleasant to walk in, and it was a good time of year. The flowers of early summer were in colourful profusion, and the trees stood gracefully about, nodding in a companionable way in the mild breeze, and the grasses swayed hushingly by the artificial lake, and children flew rather languid kites, and small knots of adults greeted each other and bowed and stopped to exchange pleasantries in the summer sunshine.

But Amelia's favourite part was the Palm House. It was an enormous and very beautiful glasshouse, glinting like a crystal palace in the sunlight.

'Oh Papa!' she said when she saw it. 'How beautiful!'

They went inside, and it was very hot – almost, but not quite, too hot to be pleasant. Great exotic plants reared their luscious heads way over the heads of the people, and created little dappled areas of tepid green shade. The earth smelt warm and rich and there was a tinkle of falling water from a tiny streamlet, over which the water-loving ferns formed a miniature green arch.

'Oh!' said Amelia again, looking up through curtainfalls of greenery, draped from over-arching branches, at the wrought-ironwork high above, held together, as it appeared, by shimmering sheets of glass. 'Isn't it beautiful?'

Edmund didn't appear to think it beautiful. He had his nose pressed to a glass panel and was looking out at some boys playing in the gardens. Grandmama didn't appear to think it beautiful. She was tugging at her wretched glove-button again. Mama didn't appear to think it beautiful. She had met some friends and was engaged in a trivial exchange of Sunday chit-chat. But Papa was watching Amelia's delight, and he smiled broadly at her astonishment.

'I thought you would enjoy it, princess,' he said. 'We may never again have a fine house with an orangery, but I thought this might do instead.'

'Oh, Papa,' said Amelia. 'It's much more splendid than a little house-orangery.'

'Am I forgiven, Amelia?' asked Papa quietly.

'What for, Papa?'

'For disgracing you, for losing our family fortune, for moving you from your lovely house and your precious orangery, for letting you all down and being a poor provider and a bad father.'

'Oh, Papa!' was all Amelia could say. She hoped she had not given Papa the impression that she thought him a bad father. She had to admit that she couldn't regard him as a good provider, but she had never thought him a bad father, not really, not even when he said things she found hurtful, or spent time in the public house. He'd stopped doing that, now she came to think of it, since Edmund's illness. That was an improvement, certainly. Still, she had to admit that she didn't think as well of him as she used to, and he was bound to have noticed.

She stepped a little closer to him, and leant her head briefly and regretfully on his shoulder. He stroked her yellow-gold hair and patted her shoulder regretfully in turn. They didn't say any more, just stood still for a moment.

'Teatime!' said Papa suddenly, yanking Edmund away from the glass wall of the Palm House, which he was in danger of pressing right through, and taking Mama on one arm and Grandmama on the other. Edmund skipped in front of the adults and Amelia brought up the rear, and together the little family negotiated the narrow, mossy path out of the glasshouse.

At the door of the glasshouse, they ran almost straight up against the Goodbody family, the parents in front and Lucinda and Frederick coming behind. In fact Edmund did run right into Lucinda's mama, his face coming smack up against her parasol, which she had lowered in order to enter the doorway.

'Ouch!' said Edmund, rubbing his nose and looking up at Lucinda's mother.

Amelia could just glimpse the Goodbodys between the shapes of the adults in front of her. Oh no! she thought, instantly running her eyes over her second-best dress, which left a good deal to be desired in the way of smartness, elegance, fashion and even fit.

'Eleanora Goodbody!' said Mama, smiling at Lucinda's mama and putting out her hand. 'It's been a long time.' And she launched into some more Sunday afternoon chit-chat, while Papa and Lucinda's father made loud friendly conversation and Grandmama smiled her sweetest Sunday smile. Meanwhile Lucinda and Frederick were hopping up and down to see over their parents' shoulders who it was they were greeting.

People began pressing on the Pims' heels from inside the Palm House, wanting to get out, and presumably on the Goodbodys' heels from outside the Palm House wanting to get in, and gradually, without actually saying anything, the two families dissolved the knot they made in the doorway, the Goodbodys stepping back a little and the Pims moving out. Other parties jostled by them, and muttered and cast irritated looks, but the two sets of parents hardly noticed that they had caused a traffic blockage.

It was only when they had moved aside from the doorway that the Goodbody children could see Amelia. Lucinda's eyes shot up and down Amelia's second-best dress, and a disdainful look kindled in them. But Frederick didn't seem to notice Amelia's dress, or to be at all surprised that the girl he had last seen dressed like a silken princess now stood before him in a rather shabby and rather tight-fitting plain dress, even though it was Sunday. He looked only into her face, right into her eyes, and, without taking his eyes from hers, he reached up and removed his Sunday hat.

'Amelia Pim, as I live and breathe!' he said gallantly. The sunlight made his red-brown hair glint and his eyes were caramel-coloured in his creamy-brown face.

'Frederick Goodbody,' Amelia replied prettily, saying not a word to Lucinda.

'My!' said Lucinda with a toss of her auburn bubbles. 'I declare, Frederick, you amaze me, remembering Amelia like that. Why, I'd have thought you met so many girls – pretty ones too – every day of the week, you'd never remember someone like Amelia Pim.'

For just a single moment, Frederick removed his gaze from Amelia's face and turned a look of intense irritation on his sister. 'Lucinda, why don't you run away and play with young Edmund here? You're acting just about his age.'

Edmund looked up wide-eyed at the sister and brother. 'Have you ever been in a train?' he asked Lucinda earnestly, taking Frederick at his word that he and Lucinda were to play together. 'I know a good train game. You make the noises and I ...'

'Oh do be *quiet*, Edmund,' said Lucinda haughtily, turning aside to examine a perfectly unremarkable lavender border as if it were an exotic specimen of great interest.

Edmund's face fell, and Amelia stretched out her hand and grasped his sticky little hand in hers, in a comfortable sort of way, but she kept her eyes on Frederick.

'Would you like to make up a party with us next Sunday?' Frederick was saying.

'I'm afraid not,' said Amelia sadly. 'You see, I haven't got a party dress. Not any more.' She hoped Lucinda wouldn't ask what had happened to it.

'No, no, not that sort of a party,' said Frederick dismissively, as if that sort of a party were the most boring thing in the world. 'I mean a walking party. Some friends and I are making up a party next Sunday afternoon, to walk along the banks of the Dodder. Papa is going to lead us, and Mama is coming along to chaperone the young ladies. Please say you'll come too.'

Amelia looked at Lucinda. Lucinda didn't meet her eye,

but went on bending over the lavender and sniffing it
pointedly.

'Lucinda can't come, unfortunately,' said Frederick in a
low voice, not sounding as if he really thought it at all
unfortunate. 'She has extra homework to do for three
Sundays in a row, for bad behaviour. She's only here today
because there is no-one at home to supervise her. Next
Sunday our older sister will be there to keep an eye on her,
so she'll be well and truly grounded.'

'Oh!' said Amelia. 'Well, if Mama and Papa agree ...'

'I'm sure they will,' said Frederick, and bowed as the adults
began to move apart, the Goodbodys back towards the Palm
House door and the Pims in the opposite direction, still
calling goodbyes to each other.

In the tea-rooms, Papa ordered tea, sandwiches and cake.
Amelia hugged her invitation to herself and almost forgot to
worry about the family finances. 'Cake!' she squeaked, but
it was a squeak that had no heart in it.

'Cake!' Papa confirmed.

The tea arrived quickly, brought by a thin, chirpy waitress,
who reminded Amelia, with a pang, of Mary Ann.

'Now!' said Papa, as Mama filled the tea-cups and Grandmama passed around the little china plates. 'I have an
announcement to make.'

Everyone looked at Papa. What could it be?

'As you all know, I work for one Richard J. Webb, in the
capacity of office clerk, a profession of no great intellectual
challenge, nor any great pecuniary reward.'

They continued to look at Papa.

'Well,' Papa went on. Then he paused.

'Oh, Papa, do get on with it!' said Amelia, breathless with
anticipation.

'Well,' said Papa again. 'Further to a recent meeting with
said Richard J. Webb, and to his review of my modest

achievements in my capacity of office clerk over the past two months, and particularly in view of the fact that I have managed to introduce a modicum of order and reason into Richard J. Webb's chaotic office procedures, said Richard J. Webb has offered me promotion to the position of office manager, on the retirement in one month's time of the present incumbent of the post.'

This was wonderful news. It meant that Papa would have a much more respectable, responsible and demanding job to do, and it meant that he would command a much better salary. But it also meant that Papa's employer trusted and respected him. Here was confirmation that Papa was an honourable man, and that there was no truth in the nasty rumours that he had acted dishonestly in his own business.

'Oh, Papa!' Amelia jumped up from the tea-table and reached over to kiss her father, but he was too far away and she only succeeded in upsetting the cream-jug.

Amelia scarcely noticed the accident she had caused, and since she couldn't reach Papa for a kiss, she blew him several across the teapot and rattled her teaspoon on her saucer in celebration. Mama smiled quietly and Grandmama merely said: 'Dear, dear, what a waste of cream!'

'What is Papa saying, 'Melia?' piped up Edmund. 'What's he saying, Mama? I don't understand Papa. He's talking too grown-up. Please, somebody.'

No-one took any notice of the little boy. Not even Mama, who had scarcely been able to keep her eyes off him since she had come home. But he must have realised that whatever Papa was saying was good, as everyone was in such great good humour, because he joined Amelia in banging his teaspoon in his saucer. Even Mama took up the clinking, silvery chorus, and the Pim family, taking tea together around a table for the first time in weeks, made a glad sound.

# OTHER BOOKS BY
# SIOBHÁN PARKINSON

## NO PEACE FOR AMELIA

When Frederick enlists for the war in Europe, the pacifist Quaker community is shocked, but Amelia is secretly proud of her hero and goes to the quayside to wave him farewell. For her friend Mary Ann, there are problems too, with her brother's involvement in the Easter Rising. What will become of the two young men and what effect will it have on the lives of Amelia and Mary Ann?

Paperback €6.95/STG£4.99/$7.95

## THE MOON KING

Ricky is put in a foster home that is full of sunshine and laughter and children of all ages. But Ricky has withdrawn from the world, and is not capable of communicating with anyone; the only words he speaks are in his mind. He has lost the ability to become part of family life. Then he finds an unusual chair in the attic, which becomes his special place. In his special chair he becomes the Moon King and finds some sense of power and inner peace. From this situation relationships slowly begin to grow, but it is not a smooth path and at times Ricky just wants to leave it all behind ...

Paperback €6.34/STG£4.99/$7.95

## FOUR KIDS, THREE CATS, TWO COWS, ONE WITCH (MAYBE)

**BEVERLY:** the bossy one, stuck up and fussy.

**ELIZABETH:** easy-going, a bit of a dreamer.

**KEVIN:** a good-looker and cool dude.

**GERARD:** takes his cat everywhere, and is barely tolerated by the girls.

**THREE CATS:** well, there's Gerard's Fat Cat, 'Fat' for short. And then there are the two Pappagenos.

**TWO COWS:** what are *they* doing in this story?

**ONE WITCH:** (maybe) well, is she or isn't she? Kevin seems to know but he's not telling. And what *is* a witch anyway?

The four, plus cat, set out for Lady Island, hoping for adventure, maybe even a little danger. But nothing prepares them for their encounter with the eccentric Dymhpna and the strange events that follow.

Paperback €6.95/STG£4.99/$7.95

## BREAKING THE WISHBONE

A group of teenagers, adrift from their families, scraping together a makeshift home in the House that Everyone Forgot. According to Johnner, it's like camping, like being on your holidays all the time. But then Johnner's just a kid. They find out soon enough, all of them, just how harsh life is when you're young, poor and homeless. The reality of living rough in a Dublin squat presents them with more difficult challenges in their already troubled lives.

Paperback €6.34/STG£4.99/$7.95

## SISTERS ... NO WAY!

*WINNER Bisto Book of the Year Award*

*A Flipper book*

When Cindy's father becomes involved with Ashling and Alva's mother, all hell breaks loose. No way will these three ever call each other sisters.

**CINDY:** if her father thinks he can just swan off and actually marry one of her *teachers*, Cindy will show him! But worse than that are her two daughters – so prissy and boring! It's gross!

**ASHLING:** if only her mother could find a nice man – but the new man in Ashling's mother's life comes with a dreadful daughter, the noxious Cindy, arch-snob and ultra opinionated.

Paperback €6.95/STG£4.99/$7.95

'Extremely clever ... Much insight and good humour ... teenage fiction at its most sophisticated'
CHILDREN'S BOOKS IN IRELAND

### CALL OF THE WHALES

Over three summers, Tyke journeys with his anthropologist father to the remote and icy wilderness of the Arctic. Each summer brings short, intense friendships with the Eskimos, and adventures 'which Mum doesn't need to know about'. Tyke is saved from drowning and hypothermia, joins a bowhead whale hunt, rescues his new-found Eskimo friend, Henry, from being swept away on an ice floe, and witnesses the death of innocence with the killing of the narwhal or sea unicorn. A story that will echo in the mind long after the Northern Lights have faded from the final chapters.

Paperback €6.95/STG£4.99/$7.95

### THE LOVE BEAN

Twins: they like the same things. But that can cause problems. Especially where boys are concerned. When Tito, a tall handsome African, walks into the lives of Lydia and Julia, it turns every relationship upside down. Then there's the 'twinny book' – *The Curiosity Tree*. It's about Sun'va and Eva: they're twins too. And a boy has just sailed into *their* lives, causing havoc. Romance mirrors romance, jealousy mirrors jealousy – it seems like history is repeating itself.

Paperback €6.95/STG£4.99/$7.95

# CHILDREN OF THE FAMINE TRILOGY

### UNDER THE HAWTHORN TREE
*Marita Conlon-McKenna*

*Illus. Donald Teskey*

Eily, Michael and Peggy are left without parents when the Great Famine strikes. They set out on a long and dangerous journey to find the great-aunts their mother told them about in her stories.

Paperback €6.95/STG£4.99/$5.95

### WILDFLOWER GIRL
*Marita Conlon-McKenna*

*Illus. Donald Teskey*

Peggy, from *Under the Hawthorn Tree*, is now thirteen and must leave Ireland for America. After a terrible journey on board ship, she arrives in Boston. What kind of life will she find there?

Paperback €6.95/STG£4.99/$5.95

### FIELDS OF HOME
*Marita Conlon-McKenna*

*Illus. Donald Teskey*

The horrors of the Famine are over, and the trilogy continues. In America, Peggy hears the call of the wild west. Back in Ireland, will Michael and Eily ever manage to get fields they can call their own?

Paperback €6.95/STG£4.99

# MORE HISTORICAL FICTION FROM THE O'BRIEN PRESS

## THE GUNS OF EASTER
*Gerard Whelan*

It is 1916: from the poverty of the Dublin slums twelve-year-old Jimmy Conway sees the war in Europe as glorious, and loves the British Army for which his father is fighting. But when war comes to his own streets, Jimmy's loyalties are divided. Looking for food for his family, Jimmy crosses the city, hoping to make it home before curfew.

Paperback €6.95/STG£4.99/$7.95

## A WINTER OF SPIES
*Gerard Whelan*

Sequel to the award-winning, *The Guns of Easter.*

Eleven-year-old Sarah Conway, Jimmy's sister, wants to be part of the rebellion in Dublin in 1920. But Dublin is a dangerous, shadowy world of spies and informants in the aftermath of the Rising. Who should Sarah trust?

Paperback €6.95/STG£5.50/$8.95

## WAR CHILDREN
*Gerard Whelan*

A compelling and powerful collection of stories set in the time of the War of Independence. Six different children try to come to terms with life during wartime, a time when neither ignorance nor innocence offer any protection.

Paperback €6.95/STG£4.99/$7.95

## SAFE HARBOUR
*Marita Conlon-McKenna*

Sophie and Hugh are left homeless when their house is bombed during the London Blitz. They are sent to Ireland to live with their grandfather. They have never met Grandfather, and their Dad never speaks of him. How will they live in a strange country, with a man who probably hates them – and will the family ever be together again?

Paperback €6.95/STG£4.99/$7.95

## KATIE'S WAR
*Aubrey Flegg*

Katie's father returns shellshocked from the Great War. Four years later the Civil War is breaking out in Ireland. Katie's family is split by divided loyalties, and she feels there is no way she can help. Then she and the Welsh boy, Dafydd, find a hidden arms cache. Can they make a difference after all?

Paperback €6.95/STG£4.99/$7.95

## THE CHIEFTAIN'S DAUGHTER
*Sam McBratney*

A story of conflict, power and first love, set in Ireland 1,500 years ago.

At a young age, Dinn Keene was fostered with a remote Irish tribe. Now an old man, he recounts the tragic tale of his first love: his beloved Frann – the Chieftain's daughter. Dinn had no right to love the daughter of a powerful chieftain, and Frann's future could not involve a boy from a family beneath her own. But they could not have foretold how much sorrow their forbidden friendship would bring to bear on them, and their tribe.

Paperback €6.95/STG£4.99/$7.95

*Send for our full-colour catalogue*